A Mirror Darkly

E. R. Vernor

Dark Moon Press

Acknowledgements

The author would like to thank the following people for their inspiration for the following tirades...

Magus Anton La Vey, High Priest Peter Gilmore, Magister Paradise, Magister Robert Lang, Magister Bob Johnson, Magister Sass, Carl G. Jung, Friedrich Nietzsche, Ayn Rand, P.T. Barnum, H.L.Mencken, Thomas Paine, Robert Greene, Partha Bose, Helen Ellerbe, Voltaire (both past and present day satirists), Plato, Socrates, Michelle Belanger, Ego Diabolus, Starr, Lady Melissa, my mentor and best friend Jack and a multitude of others...

Other works by author include:

Embracing the Darkness; Understanding Dark Subcultures, (Dark Moon Press, May, 2005)

Promethean Flame, (Dark Moon Press, Aug, 2008, 2020)

I, Lucifer: Exploring the Archetype and Origins of the Devil (Schiffer Publishing, September, 2011)

Haunted Asylums, (Schiffer Publishing, 2012)

In Memory Of

Magus Anton Szandor LaVey

(1930—1997)

Photo courtesy of Church of Satan

A Mirror Darkly Written by E.R Vernor

Design and Layout by Dark Moon Press

Published by Dark Moon Press

Copyright 2006, 2011, 2020

A Mirror Darkly is published by Dark Moon Press Ft. Wayne, Indiana

For a full catalogue of Dark Moon's publications refer to

http://www.darkmoonpress.com

Or send an SASE to:

P.O. Box 11496, Ft. Wayne, Indiana, 46858-1496

All rights reserved. No part of this book may be reproduced in part or whole in any format whatsoever without first contacting the author for permission.

A Mirror Darkly was chosen as the title for this publication because are we not a mirror reflecting the dark chaos that lies within us all? The forbidden jokes, the sharp criticism of our fellow man's incompetence, pointing out various religions shortcomings, and displaying obscene or disturbing artworks. Are all these things not the fearful nature inside us that we as society hide from? I seek to rip open the collective Shadow and expose what is contained. See me and see the dark depths of yourself...

Table of Contents

Acknowledgements 3

Introduction 15

Get Off My Lawn 19

Separation of church and State 23

The necessity for greed 31

Pardon me but Did I Offend You? 37

Entitled Much? 43

Idiocracy came early. 47

Lonely at the top… 51

The Devil You Know 61

Responsibility and the Malignment of Character 67

"Make your head go boom" 69

Pretenders to the Throne 71

Would You Like Fries With That? 75

The Lie of Altruism 85

The Weak Shall Inherit…. Nothing. 89

Why We Need To Be Elitists 93

Noah Meets the Easter Bunny 97

Satan for President 101

The Rise and Fall of Empires 113

Service With A Smile 115

Clothes DO Make the Man 119

Hyde and Seek 123

Vlad, Rise of a Satanist 131

Nature and Man 137

Misplaced 'Alien Elite' 141

Not My Glass 145

Introduction

A Mirror Darkly is the second book ever to be produced by Dark Moon Press back when I decided to do more than my first book, *Embracing the Darkness; Understanding Dark Subcultures*. So why a second printing with added content you might ask? It is quite simple. I have grown and evolved some as has the company in the last five years (as of this writing more than 3 dozen books will be produced in the next couple of years) and we have gone from a simple one title self published company to a legitimate small press. I have half a decade of education under my belt, from both several degrees and the real educator, life itself. I continue to observe my fellow man and am more aware of politics and world religion. Thus, I felt driven to add more articles into this tome of essays, such as *The necessity for greed*, *Separation of Church and State*, and others. I also added to and clarified sections of other articles. As before, it is not politically or socially correct by any means and so might offend those with sensitive skins. So be it! In order to visually reflect that mindset I have chosen to reformat the book and cover to a more somber view as I myself have become more polished in appearance. Sure, I still love the gothic (not emo, never!) old world aesthetic, but the frilly shirts have been replaced by the all black suit, corporate Goth if you will, or more dignified Satanist. I have learned from my fellow dark compatriots many lessons and a tip of the hat to Magister Paradise's writing "The power of the Black suit" for deeper understanding in *Bearing the Devils Mark*.

Nothing is new under the sun. Thoughts and ideas of philosophy have changed little over the centuries, but great men from Aristotle to Anton LaVey have radically shaken the very foundation of what the common man may ponder. Especially if for a moment we consider what the limitations of the masses' thoughts typically might be, there is little, for the most part, beyond the mundane task of getting by in life. Few ideas may be truly original concepts, but it is no excuse to stagnate. There is no shame in standing on the shoulders of giants who precede us so long as we, in turn, add to those concepts.

My purpose is not to surpass the works contained in *The Devil's Notebook* by Anton LaVey, but to relate my own views in a similar fashion befitting today's environment. My work here is a result of having opened my mind to other concepts rather than to accept blindly those force fed to me in my formulative years. Like Lucifer I am always the rebel, always the challenger. Satanists are indeed born, not made. You cannot force free thought or creativity; we can simply nurture it in fledglings among us who require little more than an example before them to prompt action.

Truly forward thinking people over the centuries have similarly nudged students in philosophical quandrums to shake convention knowing that scholars of old overlooked, or worse, held back progress of mankind by hamstringing both spontaneity and individuality. Pressures from dogmatic religions and governments alike wanting to control their populace have lead to a mass of drone-like inhabitants of our world. As a society we know for a fact that the world is round, and that reading is not only for the wealthy; but long ago thinking or teaching the things we now take for granted were punishable as crimes, the penalties often resulting in death. Challengers such as Galileo are now heroes. To some people the likes of H.L. Mencken, Nietzsche, Byron, and Paine were heroes and challengers as well. Where are such colorful, life loving, and radical misanthropes in our current times? Now, in the twenty-first century we have individuals such as Anton LaVey, who gave us ideas that shake up our worldview in a much similar fashion. Unfortunately, due to the mere choice in naming this secular and existentialist religion what he did, the revolutionary ideas presented were maligned or simply swept aside, shoved under the rug, and fully ignored for the truths he and his fellow malcontents inspired and wrote about. Millions of copies of *The Satanic Bible* have circulated the globe in many languages, but still how many recoil with a repulsed look if they catch someone in public wearing a sigil of Baphomet?

As a society we are afraid of the unknown and fear of change because we hate both with a blind passion, even if change would do us good. As if losing control over other human beings' thoughts would devastate the planet.

Perhaps the trade off for being true to oneself, demonstrated by the flamboyance of one's style of dress or ornamentation signifying their affiliations, is to be shunned. If that is part of the price for not being one of the mindless masses, then so be it… it is one I am willing to pay.

It is with pleasure that I share my thoughts. I offer no apologies for what commences, but you are warned. In the words of a Sicilian axiom, "Do not ask for what you cannot receive."

Get Off My Lawn

Spare me your collective manufactured outrage, whether it be religious based, political of any leaning, pontification on social issues as you rail your useless angst for a good guy merit badge as a whole the rabble cries with futile platitudes.

Instead, if life is so dreadful, stop posting useless memes or adding to the threads that waste time, and get off your keyboard. Venture forth in the real world and change the lives of others you claim to care about with actions, not mere words. Start at home, do self-improvement and educate morals and lost etiquette to your children, and let the ripple effect take hold as your neighborhood is free of all manner of trash. Improve your city, then state, and one by one the nation truly becomes great. Make America great? The cold truth it and the world itself never was, but with dedication, it can become that way. It is not up to an ambiguous they but in the minds and actions of us all, equally responsible for our own being.

Far too often we see the herd whine and complain. There is little to be accomplished by futile whining. I myself am equally of two minds about what to do. Part of me wishes nothing more than to amass my fortune, buy property and build a well defended Gothic mansion, stocked for both defense against outsiders, while indulging in the finer things I amass. The other part of me sees hidden potential in youg proteges, so I thinly disguise Satanic principals as a self-help author and life coach, because it is far easier to make a living as a Satanist if we don't label it as such. The praise is nice and the income is better so I theorize that I am living up to the ideals of reaching ones full potential and indulging while doing so, but we each must find our own way to adapt to the ways of the world that are unlike us. The truth of the matter is as time marches forward, we Satanists are not becoming more prevelant but rather even more becoming a minority of well adjusted, ambitious elitists. Each of us must find a way to cope with those who cross our path. For some it is to feign ignorance of our cabal of modem Hellfire Club members, others can embrace it with no harm coming to them for a public association to the infernal empire.

When I was younger, I built a reputation under a pen name and as a known Satanist and it served me well in a niche market all over the world. However I saw as I grew older and wanted to make a better living, I withdrew a bit from the public eye as a Satanist and focused on the reinvention of the self with shorter hair, nice suits, and businesses the masses could relate to without totally abandoning my roots. I surmised if I wanted to live in luxury it would take planning in order to comfortably withdraw from the world like Nemo of 1,0000 Leagues Under the Sea! You could say I am using the rubes to escape their dreadful self-imposed realties.

Can anyone accomplish this? I believe so. All one needs is a few mentors, a carefully laid plan, and the willpower to see it through.

I wish my younger counterparts well in circumventing the greater unwashed that we all grow to detest sooner or later, much like Clint Eastwood in Grande Tureano, when he famously held a Garande rifle up to the neighborhood gangbangers and uttered, "Get off my lawn."

Perhaps not all of you see the masses as cynically as I do. Yet.

Give it time. I'll wait for you to join me for Hugh Hefner styled parties in my mansion after its built.

Separation of church and State

The ludicrousness of Herman Cain as a fill in on the Neil Boortz show made me choke and spit my drink a day or two before Christmas. Mr. Cain is an American newspaper columnist, businessman, politician, and radio talk-show host from Georgia who rallies his followers to decry secular individuals and demands we all bow before the Christmas tree as he does, ignorant of the fact the Yule Log is actually a pagan custom of burning the tree. He had to audacity to say something about God not being in schools but accepted in prisons is proof we need God back in the classroom. "Why is it we can have religion in prisons but not in school?' he asked. Apparently the congressman never heard of separation of church and state. The *"wall of separation"* term has become a common expression to describe the concept pioneered in the United States that the government and churches should keep out of each other's way. When one studies religion and conflict, just about every significant conflict has had a religious dimension. The Crusades were a hundred years long. *The Dark History of Christianity* by Helen Ellerbe describes how the Church hunted down its own and waged war against the Carthers. Further proof? The Bible itself has many examples of wars in it and the slaughter of innocents that need be offered as tribute. This much needed wall between church and state strongly guarded in the Constitution of the United States, demands total separation of the church from the state, emphasize the plurality of faiths and non-faiths in the country, and the broad guarantees of the federal Constitution. What is known as 'The Lemon test" brings us more solid rules which schools, fundamentalists and secularists all must recognize. This phrase is from the case of *Lemon v. Kurtzman* (1971), the Court created a three part test for laws dealing with religious establishment. This determined that a law was constitutional if it:

1. Had a secular purpose

2. Neither advanced nor inhibited religion

3. Did not foster an excessive government entanglement with religion.

The Supreme Court has consistently held fast to the rule of strict separation of church and state when matters of prayer are involved. In *Engel v. Vitale* (1962) the Court ruled that government-imposed nondenominational prayer in public school was unconstitutional. In Lee v. Weisman (1992), the Court ruled prayer established by a school principal at a middle school graduation was also unconstitutional, and in Santa Fe Independent School Dist. v. Doe (2000) it ruled that school officials may not directly impose student-led prayer during high school football games nor establish an official student election process for the purpose of indirectly establishing such prayer. The distinction between force of government and individual liberty is the cornerstone of such cases.

Mr. Cain and those like him are so busy tearing down secular humanism they fail to comprehend their own government's forefathers were not only Judeo-Christians, but Freemasons,

Deists/Humanists and borderline Atheists. Totally hypocritical of the man who says on his radio show website that he offers to lecture on "Life, liberty and the pursuit of happiness…, Defend the Constitution and all of its Amendments" which, shocking as it may be to you sir, includes the freedom of religion. Liberty? Pursuit of happiness? Liberty would be taken away from children in choice to NOT hear God in the classroom, which is exactly why the above mentioned cases were fought. Sorry Mr. Cain but that includes Pagan, Muslim, Wicca, Satanism, and none of the above. Religion doesn't belong in the classroom unless you go to a Catholic school, a synagogue or mosque. Mr. Cain loves to quote Jefferson who wrote in the Declaration about a "Creator" as his proof on God and government. Creator is not the sole property of Judeo-Christianity my friend. The Greek and Romans pantheon, the ancient Nordic Vikings, and Babylonians/Assyrians had 'creators gods' too. Thomas Jefferson mentioned that he "it does me no injury for my neighbor to say there are twenty gods, or no god. It neither picks my pocket nor breaks my leg." It gave me pause for thought in this case with the religious right and their need of religion for morality or the fall of mankind en mass or some such nonsense. Shall we raise a temple to Aphrodite in Sex Ed class then? Roman orgies might conflict his views on morality, another concept Christians seem to think they hold the exclusive trademark on.

In fact, as far as Jefferson goes "We hold these truths to be self-evident, that all men are created equal; that they are endowed by their Creator with inherent and inalienable rights; that among these, are life, liberty, and the pursuit of happiness; that to secure these rights, governments are instituted among men, deriving their just powers from the consent of the governed; that whenever any form of government becomes destructive of these ends, it is the right of the people to alter or abolish it, and to institute new government, laying its foundation on such principles, and organizing its powers in such form, as to them shall seem most likely to effect their safety and happiness - *Declaration of Independence* as originally written by Thomas Jefferson, 1776." I would wager that Mr. Cain is not so well read on Jefferson or the others or he would know the saying "Rightful liberty is unobstructed action according to our will within limits drawn around us by the equal rights of others. I do not add "within the limits of the law" because law is often but the tyrant's will, and always so when it violates the rights of the individual, says Thomas Jefferson, letter to Isaac H Tiffany (1819).Religion has long been the sole reason for man inflicting great pain on one another. "Millions of innocent men, women, and children, since the introduction of Christianity, have been burnt, tortured, fined, and imprisoned; yet we have not advanced one inch toward uniformity. What has been the effect of coercion? To make one-half the world fools and the other half hypocrites. To support roguery and error all over the earth." Again, Thomas Jefferson, *Notes on the State of Virginia,* 1781-82 Of course more people than Jefferson made strong points against religion but I use him simply to drive home the point to religious politically motivated that their precious bedrock of ideals were built by several individuals who would be horrified at the views proposed by their modern counterparts.

And no religion in the world save Satanism holds pursuit of happiness as such a high standard of the religion! True Satanism (www.thechurchofsatan.com) and the books by the founder, Anton LaVey explains what Satanism is, as well as my own books.

To say the least, Pagan faiths love animals and nature. Pollution and animal rights would be harshly dealt with if this religion made up the laws as 'fundies' who claim to help the world so much. Satanism is evil they shouted from the rooftops during the second Inquisition, that is to say, during the 1980-1990s Satanic Panic farce that claimed Satanists were a global epidemic slaughtering small animals and children by the thousands. Do tell? if you want torture, murder and sick, twisted blood rites, you need seek no further than the Holy Inquisition of the Church of Rome. The most diabolical cult in existence scarcely compares with what the Inquisition did in the name of God like burning many five year olds in public as a witch. Former president Clinton signed the law on the Religious Freedom Restoration Act, saying "we made it possible, clearly, in areas that were previously ambiguous for Native Americans, for American Jews, for Muslims to practice the full range of their religious practices when they might have otherwise come in contact with some governmental regulation." When it comes to interpretation of the law, Supreme Court Justice Harry A. Blackmun."When the government puts its imprimatur on a particular religion it conveys a message of exclusion to all those who do not adhere to the favored beliefs. A government cannot be premised on the belief that all persons are created equal when it asserts that God prefers some."

We have to accept the dominate religion of this country is Christianity. But the majority thought does not make it correct or Lemmings would not commit mass suicide by hurling themselves over cliffs. Perhaps the screaming fundamentalists should follow their lead denigrates, insults and demeans atheism and atheists, yet wonders why atheists do the same to Christianity. If people like this want to blame someone for lack of compassion for their fellow man, let us look no further than the evangelical creationists. They started attacking science (the primary tool we atheists use instead of revelation to test truth claims) long before atheists, humanists or Satanists raised the question of faith being the answer to all life and its hardships. Science makes life easier and us live longer, more productive lives. The next time when Christmas rolls around and the cashier or door greeter wishes you a Merry Christmas, don't be quick tempered if they assume your Christian and lash out but be firm in your stance that Happy Holidays as a reply fits everyone better. Secular atheists and pagans I know celebrate with a get together for solstice or holiday parties. Those of us non-Christians will celebrate the season because of its pre-Christian roots. Feasting to raise their spirits because it's winter out, yet halfway to spring. The tree was all about gifts for natures creatures, hence the popcorn and cranberries. The lights on trees were symbols, from candles placed in the trees. Or the simple fact it's an excuse to enjoy getting gifts. As I texted a friend who loved my honesty, "May your guilt ridden and compulsive consumer driven friends and family gift you everything your black little heart desires." The end of the year reminds us of time's passing; of our mortality, and opportunity wasted, and it more importantly becomes a motivator for past mistakes. Now that's Satanic!

While Christmas is a time of year for millions to share in the joy of life, don't forget Jesus was a Jew, not a Christian whose birthday marks him as a Capricorn. On that note, I will leave you with a final quote from the man who wished for less religion in our government at any time of year.

And let us reflect that, having banished from our land that religious intolerance under which mankind so long bled and suffered, we have yet gained little if we countenance a political intolerance as despotic, as wicked, and capable of as bitter and bloody persecutions.... error of opinion may be tolerated where reason is left free to combat it.... I deem the essential principles of our government.... Equal and exact justice to all men, of whatever state or persuasion, religious or political; ... freedom of religion, freedom of the press, and freedom of person under the protection of the habeas corpus, and trial by juries impartially selected.
-- Thomas Jefferson, First Inaugural Address, March 4, 1801

The necessity for greed

"...The point is, ladies and gentleman, that greed, for lack of a better word, is good. Greed is right, greed works. Greed clarifies, cuts through, and captures the essence of the evolutionary spirit. Greed, in all of its forms; greed for life, for money, for love, knowledge has marked the upward surge of mankind... The point is ladies and gentlemen that greed, for lack of a better word, is good." ~ Gordon Gekko, *Wall Street*

It is said that pursuit of money is the root of all evil. Capitalism is an evil to other philosophers and intellectuals in remote countries. And while fools believe this, I laugh inwardly at the ideals of the have not's (or pious hypocritical 'haves' of the world) and remind myself that once I was homeless and climbed up to a point where I earned three degrees with high honors and enrolled into law school while building a publishing house that has sold copies of my work to twelve countries. I tell you this ladies and gentlemen – I have been poor in the distant past, and I have eaten at five star restaurants while in Las Vegas on a weekend vacation paid for by my hard work - and believe you me, I fully appreciate Charlie Sheen's character, Bud Fox when he said in *Wall Street*, "I never knew how poor I was until I had money." As I thought about that and where I wanted to go in life, I recalled the words of Donald Trump, who said, "I like thinking big. If you're going to be thinking anything, you might as well think big."

He makes it all sound so easy and it actually is – it is just a matter of changing your mindset.

While other people feel content being middle class or on food stamps because they choose to stay in their place lamenting (or worse being resentful of those who aren't) I struggled to master business from both college and real life, under my friend and mentor, Jack taught me to learn to think on my feet and never lose sight of the bigger picture I wanted, not to dream big but to push for it. *Never settle, he said, in relationships, quality or business….life is a business* he often said. How we chose to enjoy it or not is up to us. Jack is one of the shrewdest sharks I know but lives his life to the fullest. I joked he was a de facto Satanist often and he said, I'm just me. He was and is the best living Milton to Lomax (The Devil who taught the young attorney how to be even more demanding from life in the *Devil's Advocate*. He was my Gordon Gekko….the difference between me and the star of these movies is huge. I took the mentor by the hand and didn't quit or turn on him. My business saw a two hundred percent increase in half a year and stayed that way since his coaching. He would take me to fancy restaurants in his shiny black convertible sports car worth more than my place of living and bought me my first three figure suit as a lesson in what the finer things were. I developed a stronger sense of focus than ever before.

The following is an excerpt from Atlas Shrugged, back in 1957 by Ayn Rand.

"So you think that money is the root of all evil?" said Francisco d'Anconia. "Have you ever asked what is the root of money? Money is a tool of exchange, which can't exist unless there are goods produced and men able to produce them. Money is the material shape of the principle that men who wish to deal with one

another must deal by trade and give value for value. Money is not the tool of the moochers, who claim your product by tears, or of the looters, who take it from you by force. Money is made possible only by the men who produce. Is this what you consider evil?

"When you accept money in payment for your effort, you do so only on the conviction that you will exchange it for the product of the effort of others. It is not the moochers or the looters who give value to money. Not an ocean of tears not all the guns in the world can transform those pieces of paper in your wallet into the bread you will need to survive tomorrow. Those pieces of paper, which should have been gold, are a token of honor--your claim upon the energy of the men who produce. Your wallet is your statement of hope that somewhere in the world around you there are men who will not default on that moral principle which is the root of money, Is this what you consider evil?"

This writing stood out to me, as clear as a bell on a cold winter night it rang true to me. The various movies and books that champion a Machiavellian attitude on wealth and dealings with our fellow man served to grind in the lessons of common sense. Your friends will slowly slip away or stab you in the back; lovers grow tired of you looking for the bigger better deal as that is the primal nature of mankind. However, if earned hard and invested wisely, money will never leave you. That is the nature of the beast, as we are all looking for survival and those most fit will do so well. *The Satanic Bible* is a great book for the basic, however I *recommend The 48 Laws of Power, The Art of Seduction* and *The 35 Strategies of War* by Robert Greene, *What Would Machiavelli Do? The End Justifies the Meaness* by Stanley Bing as well as *Get Anyone to do Anything* by David Lieberman. Of course there are hundreds more and I plan on writing my own, culled from the best footnotes of these and others as well as my own life experiences in a book called *Hail Thyself! Unlocking the Secrets of Control, Wealth, and Power.* Following the logic of watching others and learning from their mistakes is priceless as it saves you the error of their ways. Get used to paying attention to the losers and the winners of the world and see through it all, once you see that there is a common denominator to all successful people in the world you can emulate them after a time. Are we all destined for greatness? Of course not. That is where stratification, genetic potential and Will to Power come into play. But we do all have the ability to reshape our lives to some degree as long as we are willing to look directly into the mirror and into our own hearts, deeply looking past what has been beaten into us as socially acceptable of ethical. Why deny ourselves what is in our nature to do? Which is, in this writer's humble opinion, to survive, above all else and to live as best as we are able to at any given moment. The harsh reality is money is what is needed to get what we want, so stop blaming anyone and everyone in the world for your lack of standing in the world and ask yourself what my mentor did. How much is enough for you? Only you will know for sure, and it may change over time. You may be ok with a certain level of income that is steady and allows you free time to enjoy other things instead of working all the time. Other people live for the rush, and work itself is not work. As Donald Trump says, "I don't make deals for the money. I've got enough, much more than I'll ever need. I do it to do it." Money makes life easier and for people that say it doesn't buy happiness, well, in the words of Gene Simmons of Kiss, "Whoever said `Money can`t buy you love or joy` obviously was not making enough money." And for my humble opinion, should you ever earn it or win the lottery you will agree with me when I say to you, it sure puts a nice down payment on it!

Although he is listed in the acknowledgements, I dedicate this particular essay to Jack, while I raise a glass of fine wine to him, and in his ideology, for myself as well!

Pardon me but Did I Offend You?

Our nation obsessed with being offended, with millions of in the indignation and can't wait for any opportunity to take umbrage at something.

Added to the unbridled enthusiasm for outrage combined with the constant saturation of news and over hyped information immediately retweeted by our fellow crybaby poor me Americans, it creates an environment where offense grows unchecked. The boredom, especially during the lockdown of the Corona Virus, was the perfect storm of unrest and hostility, to latch onto one struck match after another to the powder keg waiting to explode. These miscreants relish in it, with their warped sense of perspective, and our perverted moral compass, and suddenly you find offendedness thriving to a degree never before.

Buzzwords of the times come and go but the ones that stand out the most recently to me are 'snowflake,' and the endless parade of folks in 'cancel culture' running rampant.

"The quickest way to destroy a nation is to demonize and then penalize one group over another. Turning a generally unified nation into small burning fires of dissension and revolution. If those in power bow down to the demands of the offended, reason will eventually be replaced by the destructive nature of unchecked emotions." - *America, The Offended Nation - One Mean Dream*

If one doesn't care about owning a business, or being a public figure, sure, jump right up and write a post on social media or share a meme that will cause the younger generation to scream of inequality, of either gender orientation, racism, economic 'privilege,' or whatever else gets them attention and their good guy badges.

My utter comptempt is from people who solely spout how bad it is to have someone of color on a package is evil (suddenly) or how *Gone With the Wind* is all of a sudden condoning evils and think that *Blazing Saddles* needs a warning label at its start? Just in case you were too caught up in your own crap and missed the point of the movie portrays racists to make fun of racists. "Ridiculous trigger warning for 'Blazing Saddles' shows how far culture has gone off rail, by Kyle Smith, "When director Mel Brooks brought in a hot young black comic named Richard Pryor to help punch up the script, Pryor vigorously added in more uses of the N-word to make the movie sharper as well as funnier. Pryor may be more responsible than any other person for neutralizing the slur's power to wound." The journalist goes on to say, "A few years ago, conservatives who pointed out worrying or silly campus adventures in speech modification and idea policing were told, "Relax, it's just college kids. Why do you care?" Less than a decade later, Andrew Sullivan was able to write a column titled, "We all live on campus now," and everyone knew he was exactly right." Trigger warnings don't help students, and they might even hurt those grappling with serious trauma. That's the results of a new study on trigger warnings published in Clinical Psychological Science, yet half of all college professors admit to using them. These advocate of sensitivity, are in fact, causing more harm than good. Mevagh Sanson, a postdoctoral research fellow in psychology at New Zealand's University of Waikato, says, "Trigger warnings don't help," she said. "And they may still hurt -- the long-term consequences of avoidance have been addressed in related areas, and so we know that encouraging avoidance helps to maintain disorders such as PTSD."

The sensitivity police think everything under the sun needs a disclaimer on it to exist, if not rid the world of it entirely. This sort of labeling is not progress, it was not righting a wrong of current inequality. It's teaching people to expect that if they scream loud enough, frightened people will scramble to erase whatever they next feel is offensive bits of history as if they were unsightly graffiti on a wall. Are you kidding me, a person of color was involved in its production, back when people weren't overly sensitive snowflakes. The truth of the matter is that the cancel culture wants to rail against anything at all with manufactured outrage at the drop of a hat, over a talking maple syrup, as if it was responsible for police brutality against other races?

"Safe Spaces Can Be Dangerous" article in Psychology Today attributes even more failings in so called "Safe" spaces that "let us hide in our comfortable, little existence, which is dangerous because they prevent us from growing and changing when faced with adversity—creating new neural networks and adapting. And the ability to do just those things is what's kept us alive as a species."

The weaker and coddled we become as a society, blind us from the realities of our world. the less and less we are able to function as a mature and emotionally stable adults. We aren't able to handle the realities of the harsh world, criminals don't obey laws, so you make yourself easy prey not carrying a firearm in 'gun free zones,' absurd things that don't truly exist such as safe spaces, gun free zones, dismiss the First and Second Amendment. The very idea of free speech are under attack in America, as so many overly sensitive people believe you do not have the right to speak your mind if what you have to say might offend someone, and instead advocate for "safe spaces" in which people won't be offended by ideas they may find troubling. The 'unfriending' and family members unfollowing one another into the hundreds proves we have become so thin skinned and cannot think for ourselves.

It has gotten so bad, I post a few comments that are mildly introspective, not even close to the venom of this book, and I lose a dozen 'fans' on social media. It is so bad that I can only post images of books I am publishing or pictures of my cats, without fear that I will lose potential sales or good publicity for my events! In this day and age it seems as if no one can have an opinion at all, without first checking the news and social media to find out what the trending hysteria is of the week and latch onto it for everyone to agree with the masses sheep like hive mind.

They exist in a delusional world where they are horribly wronged victims, and everything should be handed to them on a golden platter.

They're experiencing some a deep-rooted form of denial. And their emotional distress is showing itself through their socially unhealthy behavior in public display, the proverbial child throwing a temper tantrum, but they are grown-ups doing the same on the streets of a hundred cities, month after month.

Being easily offended is refusing to grow up and accept the real world and consequences for ones actions, or lack of actions. They're so caught up with themselves, their own self-pity as reality. In this way of thinking, it's far easier to commit acts to hurt other people.

Anything to avoid the thought that maybe they're the problem.

Not looking at the real issue – the true cause, is an unwillingness to grow, think for themselves, work for what they desire and have a sense of pride.

ENTITLED MUCH?

There's a very fine line that separates self-confidence and entitlement.

expect the same rules that apply to others shouldn't apply to Entitled moochers and leeches think that they deserve respect from peers, colleagues, and even superiors, no matter what. Even, and especially if these self-serving narcissists don't deserve it.

These people, unfortunately, in the millions, are destructive, self-centered, crave attention and won't hesitate to chuck a hissy fit to get what they want as they demand endlessly, and expect everyone to be at their beck and call. They have a superiority complex gives you the notion that "they deserve" everything. Astoundingly they believe that they are entitled to everyone else's attention and efforts and can become violent when they don't get it. Quite often justifying the use of manipulative and destructive behavior as a means to achieving their demands, without compromise or debating a better way, it is their way or the highway. Riots and destruction of entire cites ring any bells?

The social justice warriors who are entitled and expect the entire world to change if they howl loud enough, have gone from their early days as tantrum throwing children who scream and throw themselves upon the ground of Walmart when mommy won't give them what they want, they are all grown up and doing it at protests for whatever giant cause of the month comes down the pipe. Insecurity tugs at the core of these narcissistic person, so they rely heavily on their fellow like-minded sycophants' compliments and admiration of the masses to both justify their unruly methods and appease their hunger for attention. These are the very same who cry for safe spaces, "the mob generation," as my friend Christina calls it, demands 'justice' without any concept of generations before it, having grown up with a slew of participation trophies and not enough ass beatings. We saw this in Seattle as a city destroyed itself in 2020, and so many others like Milwaukee, burning itself to ashes as police quit in droves. Business close, people are left to defend themselves.

There has been a seismic shift in American culture in an effort to make each child feel special. Participation trophies are almost a given, as children are constantly assured that they are winners. a cancer, spreading throughout our society and ruining the chances of future success. The lack of any sense of having to fight for what one wants leads to a lack of pride, as there is no sense of accomplishment, or even a need to excel if we are all the same. If children can't determine anything that remotely actually resembles success and victory , what will motive them to have the drive to find triumphs in medical fields to save lives, become entrepreneurs and better provide for one's family – oh, never mind, in the 'I'm entitled' world view, there is no need as we all get our adult trophies in the form of handouts, massive amounts of welfare checks, and the endless pity party merry-go-round. Who learns by winning all the time? This is harmful as it sets children up for a shock as the real world. Losing is inevitable. Everyone loses at some point in time, and these youngsters are ill prepared to deal with the consequences of something serious that they fail in.

When you're dealing with people who are selfish, make certain to speak up for yourself as soon as the person begins to step on your toes. "We teach other people how to treat us," notes human behavior expert Patrick Wanis, Ph.D., on his personal website. walk away from the situation -- figuratively, if not literally, stop spending your hard-earned time, money, and attention on them! Don't acquiesce to their demands, give them a dose of the real world. Refuse to feed the selfish person's sense of self-importance, advises psychologist Roya Rad, Psy.D.

Idiocracy came early.

People are stupid; young people are especially stupid; and we're all getting stupider with each generation. When we live in a world where the knowledge of the collective ages lies at our fingertips on a smart phone, there truly is no excuse for the state of things, outside of conditioned laziness.

Idiocracy is a 2006 American science fiction comedy film starring Luke Wilson, Maya Rudolph, and Dax Shepard, where a US soldier takes part in a classified hibernation experiment, only to be accidentally frozen for five hundred years. He wakes up to a shockingly dystopian world where dysgenics and commercialism have run rampant, bombarded by ads invading the citizens daily lives, dullard people at an IQ lower than ever and a common man is hailed as a genius to solve everyday problems becomes a hero. People are too busy procreating idiots to focus on improving their minds and smart people died off. Sounds familiar doesn't it?

If not for many facets of this film creeping up on us randomly one would think it is mere coincidence, but I suspect it is by design. Originally the term dumbing down was used as an expression in 1933 of screenwriters to mean "revising [the script] so as to appeal to those of lower education or intelligence."

The most obvious example of how Americans have been dumbed down is through our nation's failed education system. At one time we reigned supreme as a leading model for the rest of the world providing the best quality education system in the world. But over time our brainwashed asses has become a population of mindless, robotic citizenry that simply does what it's told. *The Deliberate Dumbing Down of America — A Chronological Paper Trail,* will change forever the way you look at your child's education. Written by Charlotte T. Iserbyt, is what she discovered while working in the US Department of Education and her expose on the topic.

Social media, Amazon and Facebook, our phones spying on us and pop up ads mysteriously read our minds and suggest what we buy in nonstop marketing pop ups. The public is busily preoccupied with the superficial garbage spoon-fed to the masses every single day on what are the Kardashians up to, what tragedy befell what pop singer today, via television and the internet, that all act just as effective as the most potent drug dulling the senses and the brain, as surely as mass drugs were pumped into mentally ill by the 1980s to then release an overcrowded state run mental hospitals and asylums. quick escape or quick fix for whatever ails you. Currently an incredible near 70% of all Americans are taking at least one prescription drug, alcoholism is still one of the most abused substances. lethal effects that chemically processed foods, chemical and hormone injected meat products, genetically altered organisms (GMO's) and pesticide-ridden foods that virtually the entire American population consumes. Brawno, its what plants crave right?

The masses parroting one meme and hoax after another, even saying someone famous has died when clearly, they are alive and well, raging incompetence at nearly every occupation has serious side effects. Not just food missing in an order, but full fledged near catastrophic events such as people's homes getting burned down by sloppy wiring, lazy workers, shoddy oversights by supervisors, can lead to homelessness and worse yet, death. Physicians malpractice ignored OSHA standards. Idiots at the gun range, for example. I taught two people that stand out to this day. One young woman tried to put shotgun shells in backwards, confused why they didn't cycle, another insisted her gun was unloaded yet discharged it by my thigh to prove it was unloaded and on safe.

Over numerous years a grand experiment engaging in social engineering with America's youth has been steadily working to homogenize a lowest common denominator of sub par performance out of our young, creating generations of young Americans who can neither read, write, nor think for themselves in any critical manner. According to a study last year by the US Department of Education, 19% of US high school graduates cannot read, over twenty percent of adults read below 5th grade level and that these alarming rates have not changed in the last decade, a byproduct of former President Bush's 'No Child Left Behind' math skills falling where fast food workers cannot count change back is a direct failing from public tax funded privatized programs like 'Common Core' have been sold as answering the need for higher educational standards. Coupled with a docile and obedient future workforce accelerated on steroids during the Obama administration, Trump being one of the worst public speakers with a childlike structuring of rambling speeches, the following president's idiocy after holds no more hope in my mind. The failing of our leaders, of our educational system, of lack of morality among parents who are largely absent from their child's lives is to blame.

Instead of rewarding gifted children and encouraging meritocracy, young people who are generally sharper in intellect and creativity, and are instead inadequately engaged, stimulated, and worse yet thought to suffer ADHD or other mental issues. We wouldn't want to give a trophy to a winner when it might hurt little Johnny's feelings because they never learned they should fight for what they want. No, instead give everyone a trophy to feel special., so that we have a planet full of good little employees and citizens who are then easily manipulated, controlled and subdued into the status quo of Idiocracy.

When the end result being that the thoughts of the group mind is deemed far more important than the individual mind to the extent that a person's value is only as good as the value they can bring to the whole, we are doomed as a nation, as a world. in 1970 Brzezinski wrote in *Between Two Ages: America's Role in the Technotronic Era,* the following:

"The technotronic era involves the gradual appearance of a more controlled society. Such a society would be dominated by an elite, unrestrained by traditional values. Soon it will be possible to assert almost continuous surveillance over every citizen and maintain up-to-date complete files containing even the most personal information about the citizen. These files will be subject to instantaneous retrieval by the authorities."

Welcome to Idocracy, four hundred and some years early.

LONELY AT THE TOP....

"The surest way to corrupt a youth is to instruct him to hold in higher regard those that think alike than those that think differently." ~ Nietzsche

The path of a true follower of Anton LaVey's Satanism is a lonely place at times. It is a place of detached aloofness, with few in our ranks of fellow human beings maintaining the opinion and constant mentality of being superior in so many aspects. Not many realize the effort it takes to remain vigilant of the faults of ourselves. One must perpetually remind oneself of the belief system they have pledged to, a quality lacking in weak-minded people. The cruelest taskmaster is always the self, ask any dedicated student of the arts.

It is out of our unique natures, the self awareness, and of being 'born' into it by one day waking up into the harsh world and seeing everything as it really is, without illusions. We that walk this path see the faults and frailties of our fellow man and ourselves, humanity's delusions and emotional weakness of mass mind control through politics, as well as the pious and melodramatics of people in our daily life. The masses are quite comfortable wallowing in self pity. If not, they would rectify the situation. Too many people are too fearful to break away from the mental security of routine. The normalcy of daily life is a comfort zone, and facing the actions required to push themselves is difficult if not impossible. This is the psychology factor in societies conditioning that Nietzsche hated about mediocrity.

"A human being who strives for something great considers everyone he meets on his way either a means or a delay and an obstacle. Or a temporary resting place." ~ Friedrich Nietzsche, *Beyond Good and Evil*.

When you truly realize you are different and choose to brush past everyone else, ignore the looks of resentment cast in your direction. It is almost expected of us to forgive or accept the average person's output. It is no longer noble to work hard, take pride in your work or go the extra mile. While it may be placidly condoned to be an underachiever, for some reason those who do achieve greatness and respect by their peers often become targets of jealousy or outright hatred. It is not the person those peers truly hate, or the successes of other's they despise. Rather, it is the image of themselves they abhor deep down. Those who struggle and conquer defeatist attitudes and triumph are a mirror to others of what they could be. It is far easier to talk ill of another than it is to overcome the fears and obstacles life presents everyone.

I believe the higher we push ourselves away from the average, the more alien and terrifying we become to those we leave behind. Thankless as it may be, the end results are well worth the ridicule. Self-satisfaction is far more comforting than acceptance from the masses, and should you find the means to better provide for yourself without hangers-on, count yourself fortunate. They despise what they cannot have. The longer one retains status and power, the worse the hostility may become. Sour grapes yield good wine, the older the vintage the better. Those worst talked about in their own lifetimes are hailed as heroes to a great many. Examples are Anton LaVey and Oscar Wilde the great playwright. Figures such as Lord Byron, a European dandy who although he may have been overcompensating for deformities, flaunted his uniqueness among other aristocrats but had the good sense to indulge as it suited him. If individuals such as they had not persevered and prospered, indeed, all anti-heroes would probably have become bitter angry people who wallowed in self pity. At least when you push beyond the mediocre, you can look around you in the comforts you have amassed from your hard work and be pleased with your results.

Naysayers and backbiters envy most of all what they themselves are too lazy to strive for. As Christopher Morley said, "There is only one success, to live your life your way." Revenge against one's enemies is to live well. To enjoy your continued progress while noticing your adversaries suffering is a joy to behold.

They would not give you any less quarter should the shoe be on the other foot. It is not solely for selfish purposes, I might add, that I say this. Should we not prosper so that we can provide a legacy for our families?

Inspiring the youth with thoughts that all people are equal destroys the challenge to rise above. People are not equal. Talent, labor, and virtue are forever qualities we are blessed with or chose to embrace as part of ourselves.

Some find it easier to achieve than others, due to skills they come by genetically, but it is still no excuse to give up the pursuit of excellence. In fact, when you do achieve success despite these factors, it builds an even stronger sense of pride from the accomplishment. I cannot type 10,000 words per day, but some writers can. I do however; possess the tenacity to push on despite my speed. Therefore when my biggest manuscript, prior to my first published book, the article found in these pages entitled Satan for President, became surpassed by a 243 page book, *Embracing the Darkness; Understanding Dark Subcultures*, I found myself looking back and remembered thinking that until it came off the press, I never really thought I could be an author for a living. We don't know as youths what way our lives will unfold, unless it is handed to us with a silver spoon, but once you find it, don't apologize for making it.

Use you medals, awards, what have you as motivation to continue onward. Be wary of the traitors in your midst, like Brutus of Caesar, or the men in Magus Alexander's time who assassinated their own leader. They feared them because they reached for more.

Exactly how to use logic above "morality," which is a belief based concept, for governing large amounts of people properly and how to exist in society filled with real Satanic practitioners is raised often. Lex Talionis, written years ago, remains as valid now as ever before. With this idea in mind, we must consider how important it is to create our own world to exist in, a shelter from the incessant deluge of those unlike us. A sanctuary, if you will. The following is an article written by High Priest Gilmore on

LaVey's Lex Talionis, from the Official Church of Satan, covering this thought well.

Lex Talionis

"The Church of Satan pursues a five point plan to move society in directions that are considered to be beneficial to Satanists. The first point is the avocation of general recognition and acceptance of stratification, which is no less than the elimination of egalitarianism wherever it has taken root. Mediocrity shall be identified and despised. The stupid should suffer for their behavior. The truly beautiful and magnificent are to be cherished. Each individual must choose for himself his own aesthetic standards, but we think that there are certain elements of achievement that are undeniable, even if they are not satisfying to everyone. For example, one cannot deny the undeniable, even if they are not satisfying to everyone. For example, one cannot deny the superior accomplishment inherent in a Beethoven symphony, a Michelangelo sculpture, a DaVinci painting, or a Shakespeare play. Many Satanists are working to create their own citadels of excellence outside of the cultural mainstream and have preserved the worthy from the past and continue to create new works of power to be unleashed to those who will be appreciative.

The second point is the enforcement of strict taxation of all churches. This would remove the government sanction of religion and force these parasites to live off of their own members alone, and if they can't, then they will perish as they should. The Church of Satan has never pursued tax-exempt status and challenges all the rest of the world's churches to stand on their own feet. Let us expose the vampiric nature of the organized religions and see if they can withstand the light of day.

Third, we call for the re-establishment of Lex Talionis throughout human society. The Judeo-Christian tradition which exists secularly under the guise of liberal humanism has exalted the criminal over the victim, taking responsibility away from the wrong-doer with their doctrine of forgiveness. Such thinking is a disgrace towards the ideal of justice. This must stop! Individuals must be held accountable for the consequences of their actions, and not be allowed to scapegoat society, history, or other supposed 'outside' influences. It should come as no surprise that many Satanists are part of law enforcement agencies, and a large number of people throughout this and other criminal justice systems who fully agree with Satanic philosophy on this point. If the law is not being enforced, Satanists advocate the practice of seeking personal justice, but you are warned to be fully aware of the consequences of such actions in today's corrupt society. With the present state of affairs, the outcry may yet come to welcome justice back to stay. Fourth, Satanists advocate a new industry, the development and promotion of artificial human companions. These humanoids will be constructed to be as realistic as possible, and available to anyone who can afford one. Recognizing that the human animal often raises himself up through the degeneration of another, this would provide a safe outlet for such behavior. Have the lover of your dreams, regardless of your own prowess; every man a king who can purchase his own subject; or contrariwise, buy the master you wish to serve. Freedom of choice to satisfy your most secret desires with noone to be bothered is now at hand. What could be better for blowing-off the tension that exists throughout our society, and promoting healthier interaction among true humans?

Finally we advocate the construction of total environments, technologically up-todate but theatrically convincing, to be literal pleasure domes and places of amusement and delight. We have seen the beginnings in some of the major theme parks, but let us take them on to the

> heights depicted in films like Westworld. Here you will be able to indulge in whatever environment you can imagine. Recreation of past history would not only be ripe for these constructions, but science fiction and fantasy will provide fertile sources for many of these playgrounds. Even now such projects are gearing up. The first theory is put into place by people more often than they might realize, from private schools or home schooling to promote children above the mediocre standards of public education."

Having a controlled environment allows us to be separate from the mindless herd that comprises most of the rest of society. Pleasing oneself with aesthetics such as unifying an ambience; your choice of music, art, décor, right down to your very clothing, creates a controlled environment. This frees us to focus on the things that satisfy us, to be more creative and productive. Most elitists are solitary, and find comfort in being either alone or surrounded by their friends who have been deemed worthy equals who share our sense of well being. Why waste time with those you find inferior? If you are not stimulated to the fullest, intellectually or otherwise, is it not foolish to waste precious moments of your life on ungrateful or idiotic leeches? LaVey's writings on psychic vampires are a supreme example of this. The current Church of Satan has never wavered from this stance, and all the prosperous members take this attitude to be par for the course.

Alienation from our lesser ambitious human often makes the elite feel as if we are detached from the rest of humanity, hence the term Alien Elite. Common sense, responsibility, self motivation, and drive for success are, for most people, forgotten concepts.

Eagles must build their nests in solitude. It is easier to observe the ducks below.

"We are what we repeatedly do. Excellence then is not an act, but a habit." ~ *Aristotle*

The Devil You Know

Magus Anton LaVey. A villain, a misanthrope, the devil incarnate, and to those who would follow his teachings, an admirable man. I never had the privilege of meeting him myself, but I feel I would have gotten along splendidly with him. Unfortunately, I cannot write from personal experience of knowing the founder of The Church of Satan, but it is with pride that I announce that I am a Satanist and that I put together this book as a tribute to his memory.

What is a Satanist? What does the term really mean? Many ask me that, and to better explain to people that are curious, I researched those who influenced Magus LaVey in great detail while writing this. Choosing to call this movement "Satanism" is explained later in the chapter by High Priest Peter Gilmore but I wanted to understand the thoughts of others who influenced such an individual as LaVey who has so profoundly changed my outlook on life. The more I learned, the more I appreciated his views, and expanded my knowledge. Personally, in questioning everything - as we are encouraged to do - I find myself further convinced I made the right move in allying myself to the Infernal Empire. I feel it is paramount to search for knowledge, lest we stagnate.

Among the influences of the founder of the Church of Satan was Ayn Rand, who in essence wrote that the concept of man was that of a "heroic being with his own happiness as the moral purpose of his life, with productive achievement as his noblest activity and reason as his only absolute." Her writings praised, above all, the human individual and the creative genius of which one is capable.

She exalted what she saw as the heroic American values of egoism and individualism. Like LaVey, Rand also had a strong dislike for "occultniks"; charlatans who duped many into believing they had "psychic" powers. Both despised mainstream religions, as well as compulsory charity, all of which he believed helped foster a culture of resentment towards individual happiness and success. Religious and socially conservative thinkers have criticized Rand's atheism. Many adherents and practitioners of continental philosophy criticize The Church of Satan's celebration of rationality and self-interest. Who else do we have to please but ourselves? Are we less important than other beings whom we rub elbows with? Hardly. Satanism may be selfish, but Magus LaVey was convinced that "good" is what we like, and "evil" is what we don't.

As current High Priest, Peter H. Gilmore, says in an online interview with satanosphere.com, "'Good' and 'evil' are purely subjective terms. Our beliefs and practices are beneficial to us, otherwise we wouldn't have adopted them, therefore we consider them to be 'Good' for us. Others might be frightened of our championing of individuality and our willingness to judge and be judged, based on self-chosen standards, so they might see us as 'Evil'. As ourfounder, Anton LaVey, used to say, 'EVIL is LIVE spelled backwards.' So it is all a matter of personal perspective.

We see ourselves in a Nietzschean sense as being beyond Good and Evil." He further has stated, "(Satanists) believe in neither God nor

Satan, nor any supernatural entities. We Satanists are our own gods. Satan for us is a symbol of human individuality and independence. He also symbolizes the ground of being for all existence, a hidden force permeating and motivating all that exists…. believing in either God or Satan is simply accepting a mythology that somebody else created, and thus you are in essence worshipping by proxy the person who invented such ideas.

We reject that position as being unsatisfactory; it is contrary to our nature." The good Doctor, as close friends called him, was strongly influenced by Nietzsche on theories that modern man's actions thoroughly represent the rejection of God.

LaVey dispised and vehemently opposed Judeo-Christianity, not out of being blasphemous, but out of annoyance with such dogmatic thinking. LaVey led a movement across America that challenged complacency.

As Nietzsche before him, LaVey described Christianity as a nihilistic religion because it evaded the challenge of finding meaning in earthly life. It created a spiritual projection where mortality and suffering were removed instead of transcending into something superior - in the here and now.

LaVey's religion celebrates responsibility to the responsible, and perfection of the self, where we are our own god. Adversely, the height of man's potential rarely overcomes the mentality of the bulk of slave morality, another Nietzschean concept which represents the kind of morality or ideology produced by a culture or a society.

Both men hated mediocrity and contended that the herd instinct is the inevitable consequence of our society, and that it is extremely difficult for an individual to take on a value or moral system differing from societies. LaVeys writings on elitism are much like Nietzsche's Overman – an individual who can overcome the herd instinct, who can take on values and morals not of the society they live in. In layman's terms, someone who thinks outside the box. The Overman, having overcome himself, will dominate those who have not. He is "judge and avenger and victim of one's own law", rather than that of others or one's own society. As such, the Overman/Satanist creates his own values. Both LaVey and Nietzsche defined master morality as the morality of the strong-willed. For these men, the "good" as the noble, strong and powerful, while the "bad" are the weak, cowardly, timid and petty. The essay *The Weak Shall Inherit...Nothing* found in this book, further explains why I think so. Nietzsche often referred to the common people who participated in mass movements and mass psychology as "the rabble." Valued above all else was, and still is, individualism, particularly the opposition to pity and altruism. It is very clear that in their belief only certain individuals, a Satanist in particular, should attempt to break away from the herd mentality. Another prominent philosopher who has written on the subject of nihilism, the pessimistic view of indifference as well as separation from convention, is Martin Heidegger. Views by Heidegger are regarded as a major or indispensable influence on existentialism, a philosophy of individuality and freedom, and postmodernist thinking, reintroducing traditional or classical elements of style; both philosophies radically changed much of early turn of the century thought.

A cynic to the core, LaVey was much like ancient Roman philosophers who were part of the school of philosophy inspired by Socrates. They rejected the social values of their time, often in ways shocking to those of conventional thought to prove their point. They challenged their listeners to get in touch with their natural or carnal side. Still other influences happened to be H. L. Mencken, who was a twentieth century satirist and social critic, a cynic, and a freethinker. Elitism is a belief were a selected group of people whose abilities, specialized training, or other attributes place them above their fellow man. Thus elitists set themselves apart from the majority of people who do not match up with their abilities or attributes. Elitists traditionally value intellectualism, and an appreciation of classics, such as beauty in art, literature, and music, also valued are wealth, power, and love of personal aesthetics.

One need only read *The Devil's Notebook* to see that the author viewed stratification as part of life. "Water seeks its own level" was a fond saying of LaVey's. Instead of arguing that one group was superior to another, Mencken believed that every culture, regardless of race, gender, or sexual orientation, produced a few people of clear superiority. Those born with the Black Flame burning within them are considered on par with few, which lead to a kind of natural elitism and aristocracy. "Superior" individuals, in Mencken's view, "were those wrongly oppressed and disdained by their own, but nevertheless distinguished by their will and personal achievement." Most of the aforementioned people believed in one form or another of Social Darwinism, the concept that the 'superior humans' survival is constantly at risk from the inferior man, who could 'wash away' society. Charles Darwin promoted the idea of "survival of the fittest".

This concept was echoed by novelist Jack London in nearly every work penned. Anton LaVey admired London for his works such as *Call of the Wild* and *White Fang*, which show the fortitude of man, the nature of animals, and most of all, ambition against all odds. The young LaVey must have felt a strong sense of kinship with such a novelist. Satanism is carnal, animalistic in a sense, for it embraces the natural instincts both animals and human beings have.

The so called sins of other religions would deny the basic urges we all have, for to embrace our "dark" or primal self is to abandon the yoke of our would-be masters. The Satanic Bible was written to clearly state the basic theories of humanity's unfettered needs in a common sense way. Unfortunately few people read or fully comprehend his earliest work, let alone follow through with studying the rest of his life's works.

Anton LaVey may not have been the first to speak the words of rationality so eloquently. However, he combined many thoughts into a belief system that continues to ring out loudly now and for the coming ages. If the masses fail to understand, it is due to a lack of careful examination of the truths. Those who do, and still reject us are hardly worth our time to rebuke or educate. LaVey no doubt would smile in amusement at such detractors, as anything else would waste precious time. For he lived his life to the fullest, an example to all who would follow his teachings.

Responsibility and the Malignment of Character

A portion of this article originally appeared in the author's first book, *Embracing the Darkness; Understanding Dark Subcultures.*

In the architecture and landscape of the world of how people are perceived we are placed upon gleaming pedestals or cast out among the rubble and ruin, not by the thoughts of others, but by our own actions. Mere words of others are of no consequence and have no true worth by those who accept us for who we really are. People who are swayed to and fro in their ideas of who is good or bad or right and wrong just by other's stories and opinions in conversation are dimwitted and scant attention should be paid to them. For those who know you despite all things will judge you by words they themselves hear.

To those who misjudge you, let them say what they will. A poor reputation by another's word alone dies quickly if there are no actions or evidence to support it.

Lies and truths speak for themselves. The memory of most is thankfully short, so in most cases damage is minimal. Gossip is usually just that, consider the source and weigh it for the truth it contains. That having been said, take responsibility if you are deserving of slander. In the end your true nature will win out, for better or for worse. People who commit felonious activities, cheat on their spouses or excessively lie will panic and backpedal when they are exposed to the public eye. Those most fearful of their 'ruined reputation' are deservedly anxious and paranoid. Had they concerned themselves with what lying to the audience would lead to, they might have conducted themselves better in the first place. For all things there are ramifications, and do not ever expect those you have wronged to lie still, as retribution can be either swift or lengthy in coming. To avoid this, consider the fact that when dealing with other people it always requires some level of diplomacy. Karma, in this case, is simply cause and effect, a mere chain reaction leading to poetic justice. If you find it necessary to subvert and lie, do so with meticulous detail. Let soiled hands be unseen. Control of others starts with the self. What better way to inspire followers than to excel? People want to be lead, to have a reason to exist.

We live in a disposable society, fast paced and yet at the same time lethargic. Hang around lowlifes and watch your reputation suffer for it. You are indeed judged by the company you keep.

If you cannot accomplish this then live by the following advice:

"Do not complain about that which you need not subject yourself to." ~ Anton LaVey

"Make your head go boom"

~ Foamy the Squirrel, Ill will Press

Why suicidal people should be assisted in killing themselves…..If a person truly feels worthless to society or to themselves, it becomes reality in their mind. The psyche dictates all, regardless of our sensory perceptions. Ask anyone heavily under the influence of alcohol what temperature it is, and most often they will reply that it is warmer than it truly is. I could go to great lengths telling you why this occurs, but it is not necessary for the point of this particular writing. Let us just say that chemical changes occur and the brain refutes its outer surfaces input. Words from people trying to prevent a wild eyed lunatic from playing Superman off a tall building are usually given even less validity, if they are heard at all. We believe what we are, logic and reason not relevant to emotional crisis. If suicidal people think their whole existence ceases to have any benefit to anyone, let alone themselves, they start doubting why they shouldn't just end it all. To make matters worse, while pissing and moaning, they rob the rest of us of the valuable time we have left, which we would much rather use to live as happy, productive, successful individuals.

Counselors exist to help those who actually want help prior to taking the last train early. These people should be applauded, for productive members of society should be encouraged to stay that way. Suicidal people, who refuse to get help or help themselves, have less worth than morons, for they have no excuse if they are formerly smart people who suddenly lose touch with reality. Stupidity should be painful, and ultimately stupid people should pay the ultimate price. One example of this is when you have a police stand-off with a person who claims they will commit suicide if the police come closer. Why are we wasting our money and manpower to convince this person not to do it? I say find out what type of gun they have (if this is their death of choice) and roll them the ammunition for it. Does it strike anyone else odd that the police point guns at suicidal people while at the same time telling them not to kill themselves? If we assist them, as opposed to wasting our breath on convincing them not to, we have accomplished two goals. Less whining to listen to, and they stop breathing our air!

Pretenders to the Throne

Years have past since the founding of the Church of Satan. During that time groups and individuals have laid claim to having a clearer understanding of not only the words of Magus LaVey than those he left in charge to carry on, most of whom were close friends, but attempted to change the organizations direction. Not only that, but untold numbers claiming to be Satanists with a ridiculous range of titles and denominations, mixing other faiths into its primary aspects. I have even heard of a "Gnostic-Christian-Satanist"! They bicker among themselves as to who is a Satanist or not, by what degree in comparison to each other. "So and so is no Satanist" I hear. Other Grottos, organizations, and pompous cabals sneer at true Satanists, but if they were truly as they say, would they not seek to improve themselves instead of wasting time challenging others? Are these pretenders to the throne as passionate about life, angry at our disposable society, or even understand the teachings that have brought about this theory of life? They instead miss the point that no amount of posturing will measure the accomplishments of such a unique man as LaVey? If they disagree with his teachings so much, why call themselves Satanists at all, is my query.

Start your own church with new concepts, instead of plagiarizing or bashing parts of the ideals. It is what it is. The Satanic Bible has not been reworded over the ages, unlike the doctrine of other religions, deliberately misinterpreted to suit the purposes of the "new spiritual leaders"! His concepts are in plain English, to debate them is waste of time. Agree, or disagree and go your own way.

No one forces them to be a part of the Church of Satan but themselves. Those who do carve out their own destinies use the words scribed decades ago to excel. Those lost to Satanism's truths can, if they so choose, find their way back. Errors of impetuousness or haste can be rectified. Thus we attain a step closer to perfection, by dawning realization that Satanism is about self awareness and accountability. Kooks will never gain that wisdom, preferring instead to delude themselves with the adoration of followers, more blind or ignorant than themselves, who cannot stand apart on their own. In The Secret Life of a Satanist, Blanche Barton wrote "There are no categories of Satanists – there are Satanists, and there are nuts." Devil Worshippers, to this day, give the title of "Satanist" a bad public image, like Jonathan Sharkey, Presidential wannabe and now resident of a jail. The official Church requires on the application, found on the website, that you read The Satanic Bible, agree with its Laws and Rules of the Earth. The application reads, "No one need join in order to be a Satanist, merely question herd mentality, and despise stupidity and hypocrisy." I do, therefore I am.

While striving to be perfect, use the lesser among you and your own mistakes as a measure of what not to do. People make mistakes; failure to learn from them is the real sin. I stand by my beliefs, and firmly believe that my actions and accomplishments stand as monuments of proof of my principals. I divorce myself, as much as is possible, from the mainstream as an author, an artist, and entrepreneur. Wearing a sigil of Baphomet, nor paying for the red card does not make one a Satanist. Living life to the fullest does.

Would You Like Fries With That?

Should stupid people be allowed to procreate? That has been the subject of more than one conversation with some of my friends, especially after an acquaintance of ours did one dumb thing after another. The bad part is a few of them actually have children who are just as ignorant, if not more so, than they. We propose that an I.Q. test be given to people in order to selectively breed a race of smarter human beings. If you can barely tie your shoes, your reproductive organs should be removed.

The philosopher Friedrich Nietzsche hated mediocrity in humanity, reasoning that a day will come "when there will be a superhuman race, of superior qualities." Unfortunately, Adolph Hitler took this idea, twisted and perverted it to mean kill anyone not Aryan. What Nietzsche actually meant was a race of smarter people, those who realize humanities full potential of creativity, intellect, and determination. The Ubermenvhen, as Nietzsche called it, or Overman as it is in English, was in his mind the next step in evolution of mankind. Strength and ability are governed by mental resolve with a good dose of genetics thrown in. While Nietzsche's works did influence Adolf Hitler to some degree, it must be pointed out that "might" prevailing is a Nordic tradition, which is mirrored in many other cultures. In the 1930's ideals of Western culture were torn asunder by challenges that morality is subject to personal interpretation and Judeo-Christian beliefs in unconditional love and the meek/weak inheriting the earth. Those ideals became opposed by many free thinkers who did not fall into the brainwashing of Hitler's fascist regime. Could Hitler have been an overman, as he claimed? According to Nietzsche, this is most unlikely, given that rulers represent the moralities and ideologies of their time, as opposed to breaking free from them. In his famous text "tyrants of democracy", Nietzsche opposed the covert artist's overmen to the political leaders that Nietzsche despised, clearly anti-Naziism. Is not the concept of the Overman more limited to intellectual and artistic figures such as Goethe and Wagner? This seems far more likely, especially given that Nietzsche held Wagner and such people in very high esteem early in his life. Early and current members of The Church of Satan consist of passionate, independent minded thinkers who live by the mentality that to blindly follow a leader of a group whereby freedoms of the individual are secondary to the whole is ludicrous. Satanic nonconformity is against blind mass stupidity, known as "herd mentality", being the Luciferian rebels that we are! If anything, gullible drones who quickly believe the hype that any group of the left hand path is evil fall into the category of mass mind control.

The biggest culprit is the media, who, latching onto gubernatorial candidates like "Johnny the Impaler", self styled satanic priest and vampire spokesperson, will perpetuate the myth that continues to scapegoat both parties. Mislabeled we may be, but who in reality is more free? Staring into the idiot box, (whose programming is just that, programming), teaches us to think exactly as ordered, creating the Twilight Zone feel that some master is pulling the strings behind it all. This is reminiscent of Oz's, "Pay no attention to the man behind the curtain!" Not only do we see through said curtain, we see through the actions of the man himself. More worthwhile pursuits could be had instead of wasting time watching drivel. The average school age child has seen more television than most adults have their entire lives. The box has replaced the babysitter in most households. The decline of civilization is caused by the growing number of incompetents in our youth. I am appalled to learn of our nation's growing illiteracy rates in high school graduates. Our dumbed down society has digressed to the point where The Wall Street Journal is written at a 9th grade reading level.

In a dog eat dog existence; we alphas often hear cries of unfair treatment. I feel inferior people get coddled far too much. The weakest link is what causes the strongest chain to break, grinding progress to an abrupt halt. It is the excuse whereby mediocre job performance is placidly condoned or ignored. If common sense were truly common disasters would be avoided in mass scale. However, common sense is clearly not common. In our gene pool we have the range of Albert Einstein types who can aid in seeing a man on the moon to the sad depreciation of mentality of Larry the Cable Guy. Slave morality begins in those people who are weak, uncertain of themselves, oppressed and abused. The essence of slave morality is utility: the good is what is most useful for the community as a whole. Since the powerful are few in number compared to the masses of the weak, the weak gain power via the strong by treating those qualities that are valued by the powerful as "evil," and those qualities that enable sufferers to endure their lot as "good." Thus patience, humility, pity, submissiveness to authority, and the like, are considered good.

Slave morality gives birth to values, and Nietzsche used it to described the feeling of the weak, unhealthy and ugly towards those who have fared better in life. The slave regards the virtues of beauty, power, strength and wealth as 'evil' in an act of revenge against those who have them in abundance - a classic case of what would be 'sour grapes' in laymans terms. I wholeheartedly feel that most people never achieve greatness because they are convinced by family and/or friends that they can't do things with their lives, that dreams can't come true. Many of these same people smoke cigarettes and respond to criticism by saying "We all gotta die sometime." Well, fine, let me run you over with a car if you want to rush the inevitable. If you do things for your own pleasure once in a while that is indulgence. If it harms no one else, then enjoy. But if you have no common sense, I will not pity you when bad things happen such as you get lung cancer or your body goes into convulsions from huffing paint fumes. In fact, I might pull up a chair and enjoy the show. "Watch the reject of the mental pool die folks, $1 a ticket! Buy yours fast, while he's still kickin'!"

The common denominator between Satanists and Goths is the mixture of cynicism and intellect, both having roots in the philosophy of Nietzsche - Gothic mentality says decadence is fine, so long as you are not a slave to your whims. Anton LaVey says, "The true test of anyone's worth as a living creature is how much he can utilize what he has." People who don't try due to negative influence can rise above this. Those who fail but persist anyway are courageous. Those who learn from others before committing a mistake are shrewd. Those who guess ahead as to what is about to happen, making wise decisions and gain their desired results are an inspiration to the rest of us.

The following are statistics I have learned from a researcher, in an article by M.A. Shelley-Smith, from Queensland, Australia, on the subject of stupidity:

The German department of education has the statistics for their country. Between 1890 and 1940, they have observed a loss of intelligence of 10 %. This means a diminution of the general ability down to one sixth, a diminution of the talented to one-half. In contrast, the amount of mentally-slow persons has tripled. The mentally-retarded increased four times, and there are thirty times more half-idiots than during the time of the Renaissance. The loss of one's intelligence is equivalent to a death sentence.

For our great-great grandparents, it must appear that today's so-called intelligent man is rather a dull person. In these times, our genius is hardly ever challenged. Creative acts are performed by a minority with creative power. What originally made humans human was the creative force within. We can see it in any political arena, how weak and uncertain the decisions are; or in science, how a repaired instrument just gets worse after it returns from the repair shop.

This has given the brain its stability and structural thinking patterns…In the United States in 1970, there were 40 million people that sought medical help because of emotional disturbances. Half of the United States is suffering knowingly from one or other mental disturbances and the outbreak of violence. In large towns like London, there are 30 idiots for every 1000 citizens. We can observe that the performance in schools shrinks from year to year. Now there are already first-graders using the help of teachers at home. The German educational department mentions in 1978, that in Hamburg, of 2000 children of the age of six, 55% suffer from important emotional disturbances, 20% have anorexia, and another 20% have sleeping problems.

Furthermore, a recent blog online by a teacher berating her students caught my eye.

Pa. teacher strikes nerve with 'lazy whiners' blog

By PATRICK WALTERS, Associated Press Patrick Walters, Associated Press –

FEASTERVILLE, Pa. – A high school English teacher in suburban Philadelphia who was suspended for a profanity-laced blog in which she called her young charges "disengaged, lazy whiners" is driving a sensation by daring to ask: Why are today's students unmotivated — and what's wrong with calling them out?As she fights to keep her job at Central Bucks East High School, 30-year-old Natalie Munroe says she had no interest in becoming any sort of educational icon. The blog has been taken down, but its contents can still be found easily online.Her comments and her suspension by the middle-class school district have clearly touched a nerve, with scores of online commenters applauding her for taking a tough love approach or excoriating her for verbal abuse. Media attention has rained down, and backers have started a Facebook group.

"My students are out of control," Munroe, who has taught 10th, 11th and 12th grades, wrote in one post. "They are rude, disengaged, lazy whiners. They curse, discuss drugs, talk back, argue for grades, complain about everything, fancy themselves entitled to whatever they desire, and are just generally annoying." And in another post, Munroe — who is more than eight months pregnant — quotes from the musical "Bye Bye Birdie": "Kids! They are disobedient, disrespectful oafs. Noisy, crazy, sloppy, lazy LOAFERS."

She also listed some comments she wished she could post on student evaluations, including: "I hear the trash company is hiring"; "I called out sick a couple of days just to avoid your son"; and "Just as bad as his sibling. Don't you know how to raise kids?"Munroe did not use her full name or identify her students or school in the blog, which she started in August 2009 for friends and family. Last week, she said, students brought it to the attention of the school, which suspended her with pay. "They get angry when you ask them to think or be creative," Munroe said of her students in an interview with The Associated Press on Tuesday. "The students are not being held accountable." Munroe pointed out that she also said positive things, but she acknowledges that she did write some things out of frustration — and of a feeling that many kids today are being given a free pass at school and at home. "Parents are more trying to be their kids' friends and less trying to be their parent," Munroe said, also noting students' lack of patience. "They want everything right now. They want it yesterday."

Sandi Jacobs, vice president of the National Council on Teacher Quality, said school districts are navigating uncharted territory when it comes to teachers' online behavior. Often, districts want teachers to have more contact with students and their families, yet give little guidance on how teachers should behave online even as students are more plugged in than they've ever been.

"This is really murky stuff," she said. "When you have a teacher using their blog to berate their students, maybe that's a little less murky. But the larger issue is, I think, districts are totally unprepared to deal with this."

Munroe has hired an attorney, who said that she had the right to post her thoughts on the blog and that it's a free speech issue. The attorney, Steven Rovner, said the district has led Munroe to believe that she will eventually lose her job. "She could have been any person, any teacher in America writing about their lives," he said, pointing out that Munroe blogged about 85 times and that only about 15 to 20 of the posts involved her being a teacher. "It's honest and raw and a little edgy depending on your taste. ... She has a deep frustration for the educational system in America." Rovner said that he would consider legal action if indeed Munroe loses her job. "She did it as carefully as she could," he said about her blog. "It's so general that it applies to the problems in school districts and schools across the country."

I for one applaud this educator. An instructor cannot motivate the lazy, nor inspire the clueless if they chose to stay ignorant. The old comment of leading a horse to water but you can't force it to drink springs to mind.

Intelligence and feeling are very closely linked. It is not surprising that in our time there are so many people suffering from violent emotional pain. The brain is the commander of everything. When we destroy the brain, we basically destroy humanity, which depends upon brain-power at all times.

Modern technology may indeed yield us more time, but what good is it if the time garnered is wasted? The true purpose of modern technology is to free us to use what we have more productively, and allow for down time to relax and enjoy our just rewards, not slip into laziness. Convenience breeds more laziness in less than ambitious people. Ever notice the average patron of fast food restaurants? They may vary in age and ethnicity, but consist of two distinct classes. Poor and undereducated who cannot afford better, or business type professionals who haven't the time to enjoy the life their monetary gains have brought them. Worse still are the employees of such places. The ones who year after year remain at these jobs; "lifers" they are termed. This group seems to be mostly made up of high school drop outs, convicts and welfare recipients content to never pull themselves out of their predicament. For a time I worked in the restaurant industry as a temporary solution to financial problems. I saw first hand what went on and who did what behind the counter. What irritates me most about them are the ones who wail about their lot in life and yet chose to do nothing about it. If you are content with your job, fine you are doing what makes you happy, but to complain for a decade that you could do better yet don't bother to try to find better, is pointless. If you can enhance your life but have chosen not to and are unhappy about that then it is the fault of no one but yourself. Years later I shake my head noting that as our country slowly becomes as oppressive as we have thought of other countries and we slip into a Marxist communist ideology with "Big

Brother" watching our every movement, such apathy of our overall condition spirals into an acceptance where everyone gets treated the same, regardless of output. In times past, the wearing of a tie in a restaurant indicated a sign of earned position, of rank, showing both customer and coworker alike who was in charge and more competent. Now ties are becoming part and parcel of the beginning crew member's uniform, from cashier to lobby attendant, all the way up to manager.

Neither laws nor practicality allow for the intelligence quotient as a measured excuse to sterilize, or to commit homicide. It is better to be of use than useless, at least in some capacity, no matter how mundane. So, instead of shooting the employee at the counter for his waste of space while they annoy you with their incompetence, bear in mind the use of such individuals. Should you feel the urge for a greasy cheeseburger, remember the bottom feeders have their place. After all, who else would ask you, "Would you like fries with that?" If we had to do everything ourselves, we'd never get great things accomplished or enjoy the moments we have if not for stratification.

The Lie of Altruism

It has been said "no good deed shall go unpunished". What exactly, then, qualifies as a good deed? An unselfish act devoted to the recipient alone? Let us closely examine that. "Unselfish" is typically an adjective which is used to signify that the "ego" receives no gratification, without any compensation – a false perception due to the fact that every act, no matter how one wishes to lie to themselves, has a gain for the giver. The guiltiest of such lies are the most holy. Those who make great gestures to portray that they look for no reward, laying claim that it is for the greater good, such as for orphans, for the poor, for starving nations, etc. From a nun all the way up to the pontiff himself, these "selfless givers" gain much more from this sentiment than they would want you to believe. Churches amass staggering wealth and are not taxed, although the Mormons bring in 3.8 million a year alone. The Catholics are the wealthiest of all, yet do little for the world's poor, placing the burden on the taxpayer via our Christian government. The Vatican is worth billions in land alone, not to mention the holdings on it. They gain recognition among their peers, and most of all, keys to "the kingdom of heaven." If their belief is to be given a shred of hypothetical fact, in the grand scheme of things the suffering here on Earth is fleeting compared to the vastness of eternity…so an endless existence in the glory of Heaven in comparison is what? A small entry fee to a big prize they covet. While we sinners languish in torment, they reap endless rewards, according to Judeo-Christian dogma.

Unselfish, indeed! Collectively speaking, most people would like to think of the "old days" as simpler times when life was full of good upstanding citizens, the image of a WWII enlistee with a flag waving behind the soldier. Altruistic as these

Christian patriots would have you believe they were while reminiscing about times past, The History Channel and modern authors are now challenging these falsities. The horrors of Nazi death camps went unhindered by the Allies and the Vatican despite aerial footage years before its liberation as Jews, an earlier scapegoat of the world's troubles, were slaughtered by the thousands daily. Billions of dollars in artworks, silver and gold filtered through Europe by way of those not wanting to get involved, yet they certainly did profit from the suffering around them.

Did the Church not recently apologize for refusing to lift a finger to save them? Is allowing a horrific crime to go unchecked not as bad as participating? LaVey commented in *The Devil's Notebook* that the same people who bitch and moan about crime are the same self serving "good-guybadge" wearers who blatantly ignore the elderly woman being mugged. The illusion of the 40's and *50's Leave it to Beaver* world is shattered when one realizes that war was as ugly on both sides as "the good guys" hide their involvement or lack of thereof. When we are reminded of the Japanese internment camps here in America, the tears over *Schindler's List* seem a cruel joke. If the Jewish Nazi did spare his fellow Jew by placing them into work detail, why not be more altruistic and save untold numbers by ratting out Hitler years before? I feel it was to clear his conscience and take a less troublesome route. Third side perspective is to see the truth in the middle, not buy the romanticized ideal world painted by our patriotic history books. What then of the more secular individuals, such as the common man or large corporations, whose donations go to charities of many types? They gain recognition also, an ego boost from the praise, their companies get good press (hence more income) and they get tax write-offs to boot!

Investment strategies, such as stocks and bonds, play a large part in "selfish" actions of big corporate America down and even Joe Shmoe, who craves his "good-guy merit badge" and an inflated ego. I used to believe in altruism to a degree. But then again, I used to believe in the tooth fairy and Santa Claus when I was a young child too. So when you see people strutting about proud of their good deeds, ask yourself who gains? What's in it for them? When doing for others, keep in mind the need to keep your eyes wide open. View everything clearly. At least honest people can say "I did this because it made me feel good." Bravo. That would be a partial step in admitting the truth. It is a giant leap to say altruism is a lie, and we do what we do because, deep down, it benefits us.

THE WEAK SHALL INHERIT.... NOTHING.

A portion of this article originally appeared in the author's first book, *Embracing the Darkness; Understanding Dark Subcultures*. The core of Satanism is not in responsibility, but something deeper. It is pride, and allowing success or failure to be attributed to oneself. We of the left hand path never expect anyone to shoulder our burdens nor do we fuss when another is unable to assist us in a given task. We accept the problem as our own and are courteous to those who have helped us. A true friendship, with no strings attached, is a rarity. Any sense of pity or caretaking, let alone whining about the lack thereof, is totally disgusting, humiliating, and proves the complainer is not worthy of a shred of respect. Anton LaVey wrote, "Nobody gives a shit about anyone else's grievances. When one caterwauls his troubles to another, it simply weakens the complainer in the

listener's eyes". When someone's life has taken a severe plunge into a downward spiral, it is not your job to give advice, give financial help, or anything that does not benefit you. Family loyalty often blurs into feelings of guilt leaving the real victim feeling as if they have been used beyond necessity simply due to the fact that they "had to". Assisting others because it makes you look good, if the

time given is unimportant to you, is fine if you feel it may be appreciated and someday returned. Only you know who will and will not fall into what category. Those who fail to live their lives without taking care of themselves fully, who would use you out of laziness if you let them, are known as "psychic vampires". LaVey coined this term in the late 60s, not to be confused with the second use of psychic vampirism as seen in the chapter from *Embracing the Darkness: Understanding Dark Subcultures* entitled

"Vampires Among Us," and in *The Psychic Vampire Codex*, by Michelle Belanger (in reference to Belanger's usage for psychic energy vampires). People who do so are weak, lacking their own will, drive and personal ambition. The increase of such behavior continues while those devoted to self-improvement seem to decrease. Christianity places emphasis on pity, but does this not lead to the elevation of the weak-minded?

Nietzsche believed that it was wrong to deprive people of their pain, because it was this very pain that stirred them to improve themselves, to grow and become stronger. It would overstate the matter to say that he disbelieved in helping people; but he was persuaded that too much Christian pity robbed people of necessary painful life experiences. Robbing a person of his necessary pain, for Nietzsche, was wrong. He once noted in his Ecce Homo "pain is not an objection to life."

According to Nietzsche, the Cartesian proofs for the existence of God are all examples of logic only a master from the nobility would invent. Thomas Aquinas's notions of what constitutes the "good life" is a particular example of what "good" might mean to a master. Nietzsche argues that Jesus transcended the moral influences of his time by creating his own set of values. As such, Jesus represents a step towards the overman. Ultimately, however, Nietzsche claims that, unlike the overman who embraces life, Jesus denied reality in favor of his "kingdom of God'. Jesus's steadfast refusal to defend himself, and his subsequent death, were logical consequences of his actions to create a self-fulfilling prophecy. Nietzsche criticizes the early Christians for turning Jesus into a martyr and his life into a story of the redemption of mankind in order to gain power over the masses, finding Christians to be cowardly, vulgar, and resentful. He argued that Christianity had become more and more corrupt, as successive generations further misunderstood and misinterpreted the life of Jesus. By the 19th century, Nietzsche concluded, Christianity had become so worldly that it became a parody of itself. It became a way of controlling the masses rather than a philosophy of love.

"Physiologists should think before putting down the instinct of self-preservation as the cardinal instinct of an organic being. A living thing seeks above all to discharge its strength – life itself is will to power; self preservation is the onlyone indirect and most frequent results."~ *Beyond Good and Evil,* Friedrich Nietzche

I am a champion of individual struggle and self realization. I do not concern myself with mass movements or political parties that barter or quarrel for power. I recommend that those of us that are capable be aloof, overcoming the great nausea assosiated with nihilism that overcomes most others. Become the ship Nietzsche said that "sails over morality" and be the one who endlessly affirms your own existance. Initially we must become a destructive force, excising and annihilating the insidious "truths" of the herd, and reclaim the chaos from which pure creativity is formed. Destruction is not "evil". It is part of the natural cycle of life, as is creation. It is this creative existence that justifies suffering without displacing it in some fictitious "afterworld." Become the lightning which brings ecstasy to Earth. For it is in this pain that triumph lies and that is the foundation of much Satanic philosophy.

"What does not destroy us…makes us stronger." ~Friedrich Nietzsche, *Maxims of a Hyperborean*

Why We Need To Be Elitists

A portion of this article originally appeared in the author's first book, *Embracing the Darkness; Understanding Dark Subcultures.*

Mediocrity and regrets are our only Hell, and accepting our awful fates is our own stupidity. Heaven is always within our grasp, one need just to reach higher for the next prize. Being around other likeminded people who seek better in life will encourage us to strive for more, whether it is of riches, companionship, quality, looks and/or intellect. Each acquisition knocked off the list will only encourage the individual to strive for more. However, I do not mean to say "Keep up with the Joneses".

Attempting to be what everyone else is shows ignorance of an enormous magnitude, for no two people have the same income, wants, or outgoing expenses. Live a balanced life. Use common sense, as opposed to blind greed that leads to stupid errors and often will cost everything you have gained. Blind ego is equal to blind stupidity. Proud, and rightly so, are the few who struggle as elitists, especially those who do so for their legacy, their children. What would Gene Simmons and Arnold Schwarzenegger's children be like if their parents had not moved to "The land of opportunity"? How pathetic is it that poor people from elsewhere gain so much here when we who dwell here do nothing more than sit around daydreaming about being "somebody"? Churchgoers are told that the love of money is the root of all evil. If so, why do all churches want it? Pride is not a sin, nor envy. Elitists know that it is the lack of wants that is the root of laziness, stagnation, and failure. One must take pride in themselves, or be guilty of another sin – Sloth. Not having pride in one's appearance prevents friends and employers from wanting you around. The consequences of that should be obvious! Pride makes us want better than the Joneses, if we are clever enough to amass wealth or at least appear well off enough to look worthy of having others around us. A friend of mine commented while discussing differences in life appreciation among varying types of people who have the habit of complaining about her level of indulgence said, "Why should I have to compromise who and what I am for the inability of others who cannot or will not rise up to my expectations?" Well said, Lady Melissa.

Envy of others spurs us on to acquire that which we desire; else we never get better quality cars, furnishings or the ability to properly entertain our friends or ourselves. How is that evil? Living in a hovel as a monk is fine and dandy if your friends are rodents and cockroaches! You don't have to be a millionaire to be happy. What I'm saying is do what makes you happy as long as you harm no one.

Whether it be money, intelligence, family, or whatever else makes you happy. If you envy others that have what you "have not" then make the changes in your life to make yourself happy.

If all our natural instincts lead to "sin" then at least you can enjoy your life as it is in the here and now. The desire to be intellectual promotes education. Who wants to be surrounded by idiots?

Intelligent people who think for themselves soon seek answers outside the box and question the rule makers. We are the makers of our own destinies.

"Blessed are the bold, for they shall be masters of the world — Cursed are the humble, for they shall be trodden under cloven hoofs! Blessed are the mighty-minded, for they shall ride the whirlwinds — Cursed are they who teach lies for truth, and truth for lies, for they are an abomination!

Blessed are the valiant, for they shall obtain great treasure, Cursed are the gazers toward a richer life beyond the grave, for they shall perish amidst plenty!" ~ Anton LaVey, *The Satanic Bible*

Noah Meets the Easter Bunny

I ran across an interesting point in researching various biblical discrepancies, and decided to write about Noah and the great flood. The fact is, so many people read the bible and overlook the obvious truth. It was written by human beings who are fallible, egocentric, and guilty of embellishing anything to serve their purpose. As a coworker said to me, King James commissioned the church to translate the bible to be understood by more people, in English, as opposed to earlier writings in Aramaic, Hebrew, and Latin, (supposedly) with instructions to leave the wording as it was. Now, if you were in a position of power, being as human as he, would you not take advantage of this opportunity to reword subtle parts of the "good" book in such as way that the populace did things or believed ideas YOU wanted them to? That is precisely why the wording that read "suffer not a poisoner to live" became "suffer not a witch to live" resulting in the Inquisition, in which over 100,000 so called "heretics" were burned alive, guilty of a crime or not. Great change can come about by small words. The pen is truly mightier than the sword, for it dictates who will swing the sword and in what direction.

Now, back to our fable's little discrepancies. The fact that the bible is considered totally true and not a recognized book of fiction created to teach in the form of parables, leads to the opinion that there are no flaws or contradictions. In fact there are two distinctly different variations of the story of the flood in Genesis — one is true or both are false. But if only one is true then why have the second misleading parts that people overlook? In Gen. 6:19 it states that two of each kind of animal were brought aboard the ark, yet in Gen. 7:2-3 it reads that they took seven pairs of each animal. Did they reproduce so quickly while coming aboard? How big did he have to build the ark to house them all, plus store food for all of them to consume, especially over the duration they had to remain there? Did he borrow Santa's sleigh to ferry the food in his magic bag? How did he prevent the carnivores from eating their natural prey? "God" instilled this drive within them, so did he negate it for the purpose of this rescue?

According to the scriptures, that Noah built this boat prior to the collection of these creatures. Did he give them all sleeping pills to provide protection for his family? Speaking of his family, this leads to still other questions. Did his entire family live to hundreds of years of age in order to collect all of the animals in time? Keep in mind, even up to Columbus's time in the 1400's, humans did not know of America as we are taught in school, nor of South America, or Japan or China until Marco Polo's voyages. Do we believe basic education that says NOBODY knew of the thousands of animals and insects vital to life for the indigenous inhabitants here to evolve from; or do we live by the thought that Noah, with God's divine plan, teleported himself to ALL those continents prior to future expeditions where he scooped the animals up and went back to the Ark? All aboard the crazy boat, last call!

Let us suppose then that the raccoon doggiepaddled from America (after traveling from the Midwest to the seashore), bumped into Ling Ling the panda, discussed latitude and longitude, and set out to meet the original coast guard captain, Noah. Did God erase Noah's knowledge of these creatures that mankind would not even hear about until after Leif Erickson's time?

Ok, my crass comments, having been thrown out there for my own amusement, are finished. I clarify the reasons for my disbelief as follows, in a rational manner.

No amount of time distortion could have accomplished all this, calculated all of the requirements to accomplish either the ark itself, accommodate the various elements needed, or gather every species of animal, food requirements, or sanitation for the humans to live with them all.

Archaeological discoveries contradict fundamental beliefs. It is these fundamentalists who, in order to sway us to the "rightness of God's word", try to twist outside evidence to support their theories told to those of us who remain skeptical. In Time Magazine on July 5, 1993 it read "CBS airs fraudulent archaeology special in 1993". The "Ark" wood turned out to be contemporary pine soaked in juices and baked in an oven. The fact that Gen 7:12 and others tell of the flood lasting 54 days is contradicted in Gen 8:13, 13, and 16 to the equivalent of one year. Fundamentalists who ignore these differences usually try to harmonize the passages by eliminating written words in their own dogma when repeating it to children as Noah took 2 of all critters on a big boat for a long time just because God told him to in a dream, because it is easier for grownups to simplify the story to avoid drawing obvious attention to truths. Ignorance by choice is culpability with malice aforethought.

Ponder this, if you question the beginning of a thousand page book at its first chapter for being false, why would you bother believe the rest let alone keep reading? Never underestimate the power of stupid people in masses. Apparently 1.8 billion Catholics and Christians alike would have you believe that Easter is a time to celebrate a dead man rising from his grave (zombie?) by decorating everything with bunnies and duckies and searching for colored eggs, but of course, this has nothing to do with the Pre-Christian Pagan fertility celebrations. Ahh, but that's another article in the future…

"Control, religious or political, must exist because the populace demands to be enslaved. Only when it feels sufficiently enslaved can the dissenters produce their collective grunt. Dissension is a weak form of assertion. Assertion is a weak form of creation."~ Anton LaVey

SATAN FOR PRESIDENT

"Better to reign in hell than serve in heaven." ~ John Milton

It has been said that society has created monstersbut I believe we are monsters for whom society waits. It is easy to blame society, as a massive ooze of vileness and corruption, for the wrongs individuals choose to commit.

The individual, each with his or her own agenda, flaws, and hidden guilty pleasures, makes up our society, government, and media. A Satanist proudly wears who and what they are on their sleeve, kowtowing to no one and building empires or squalor by their actions or inactions, blaming no one for their faults. Marilyn Manson has said, "You spoon fed us Saturday morning mouthfuls of maggots and lies disguised in your sugary breakfast cereals. The plates you have made us clean were filled with your fears. These things have hardened in our soft bellies. We are what you made us. We have grown up watching your television. We are a system of your Christian America, the biggest Satan of all. This is your world in which we grow. And we will grow to hate you". This quote seems contradictory to my opening statement but the point that I am making in including it is thus: Children live what they learn. If this is all they see in our society this is what they learn as the "right" way to live. It is only as we grow older that we learn to think for ourselves unless we are the fortunate few who are raised by parents who have had the wool pulled from over their eyes.

If Satan truly rules the Earth, and most claim that Satanists are his followers, should we not run society? Should the meek, the humble, and those who look to heaven for answers stop pushing their views, rules and earthly punishments upon us and allow the mighty-minded the throne? After all, their reward is in Heaven, not here on Earth.

In their belief system it says suffering places one closer to God by enduring hardships. Good Christians that do exist in our world aren't the ones who spout intolerance, they believe in live and let live; allowing us our faults and so called sins thinking that faith and the judgment in the afterlife are not for them to decide. Instead, goody goody white male dominated Christian America strove to enslave the Blacks, oppress women (who had no rights but to obey until the amendment to vote in the late 1800's), and treat the native inhabitants as servants or something to be eradicated from the earth if they did not conform to herdist mentality. The people of Asian and Irish ethnic group were treated not much better than slaves, many were indentured servants who had to work all their lives under the wealthy who paid for their families' safe passage to America.

Freedom existed, yes, for all who could afford it. It is in this light I propose a Satanist could fix five of our society's greatest failures. The first of which is fundamental to each and every one of us; education. This country prides itself in being open minded, free, and oh so Christian. However, people forget that its religious roots also hold a major reason for censorship because of prudish standards reducing expression. Aristotle taught Alexander the Great to reason and understand his opponents, a key to being powerful in the world. One cannot be educated on all aspects of the world as a whole without experiencing "offensiveness" in art (even if some call it pornography) or music which uses subcultural references, slang and crude language. This simply shows that words alone can have power over us. Can we not make our own decisions as to what is moral and what is not?

The church, during the Dark Ages, felt that writing and reading led to free thought. This would have undoubtedly led to questioning aspects of their dogma.

Thus, the Pope made it a crime punishable by death, for the layman to be caught reading or in possession of a bible.

Translations of the Bible into common Latin were not found in the hands of common individuals for centuries and the man who penned the book for the masses was dug up centuries after his death, his bones broken, cursed and burned to ash. This sounds like a Satanic ritual of destroying an enemy to me.

From 500c.e. to 1000c.e, an early implementation of early censorship laid waste to scrolls, art, and technology. Would you believe that ancient civilizations had running water as well as heating? A gloating Father St. John Chrysostom declared "Every trace of old philosophy and literature of the ancient world has vanished from the face of the earth." while standing outside the burning ruins of a library containing 700,000 books. An orderly, civilized society existed prior to Rome, and due to this destruction the world as we experience it (with a judicial system, senate, medical school, running water, irrigation and superhighways) did not come about until the 1400's to the 1800's - flawed though our system is.

Not allowing a nipple to show in a local college's newsletter is ludicrous, for is not college the place our educated are supposed to express themselves the most, to bring culture and creativity to the people? Was the PMRC (Parents Music Resource Center[1]) truly necessary to protect our teenagers in the 80's and 90's from sex, drugs and everything rock n' roll stood for? Give adolescents some credit for being able to discern for themselves what should be done or not done with their lives. Coddling our youth does not prepare them for what adults do daily, and elders often are the ones who, by example, make ruin of their own existence and are poor role models. Wisdom does not come with age, but rather from experiences that can come at any

[1] The Parents Music Resource Center was a committee formed in 1985c.e. by the wives of several congressmen in America. They claimed that thier mission was to educate parents about "alarming trends" in popular music. They alleged that rock music glorified and encouraged violence, drug use, suicide, and criminal activity. The group sought the censorship and/or rating of music. age. Experience comes from mistakes and mistakes come from experience.

This brings me to the second point of what needs scrutinized and eliminated from our country; the hidden double standard of separation of church and state. It is a myth. People are fighting to have prayer put back into our public schools. This clearly flies in the face of separation of church and state. This country claims Freedom of Religion but there are some who pound their chests and proclaim we

are better than other countries because we are a "Christian Nation". They would have us put the Ten Commandments into courthouses rallying that our laws are based upon them. I would like to think our laws are based on common sense, but alas.

As was stated in the previous article, *The Lie of Altruism,* churches are among the wealthiest organizations and do not pay taxes. I strongly support LaVey's argument that we could tax the church into the Stone Age and pay off the national debt with what the government would receive.

Jesus was poor. Buddhist monks value wisdom over material wealth, and monks of old felt poverty and suffering brought one closer to God and away from Satan.

In the year 500c.e, the vast majority of heating systems (as well as sanitation methods such as flushing toilets) were abandoned because they were conveniences that were selfish and took one further away from "God".

This caused outbreaks of death from diseases that had been long dormant. All this because it was thought one should not have issue with sleeping on a hard bench or damp earth, because to simply be indoors was luxury enough!

Over the years child molestation has run rampant in many churches, and when pressed to take a stance against it due to public outrage, the Pope backpedaled from trying the accused. It is far easier to condemn sex for centuries and sweep these incidents under the rug (or give pity to the vile individuals who committed these atrocious acts) than to examine the leading cause of the sexually frustrated to become deviant predators. This in no way excuses such predatory actions, but rather helps in explaining the manner in which the overall psyche was shaped within the church.

This brings me to the next subject of change; crime and punishment. I believe in fair trials, not the farces of corruption that plague our system. It is our duty to protect those we care about with swift and harsh vengeance, lest these wrongs go unaddressed. All persons should defend themselves if able. Cross country concealed permits for handguns should be issued in much the same manner as vehicle licenses; show capability in its use then allow the person the right to use it. I advocate it be a one time fee revocable only if found guilty of criminal use with it. Indiana has a bill pending as of this writing to a similar permit, a lifetime permit. Hopefully this will pass and influence other states' legislators to follow suit. Use the weapon that best fits your capabilities as well as the most lethal ammunition available, and practice. Too often a new firearm buyer leaves their weapon untouched in a bedside table or somewhere comparably out of sight and out of mind, and then become victims due to unfamiliarity.

Far too many prisoners are on death row for decades, and have cost taxpayers well over $60,000 per year. Such an astounding amount of cash should, instead, go to the victims' families as restitution for their loss. A bullet, after all, only costs three cents to execute them.

Work release and community service could take care of the overcrowding problem. Hire more guards creating more jobs to watch inmates. Let us put breathalyzers in all car ignition systems. It does not disallow a person from becoming intoxicated; it simply encourages them to do so only to the point of enjoyment, and full control of their vehicle. No one should lose their life at the hands of a drunk behind the wheel. This would force responsibility onto the stupid people of our world. One should indulge instead of abstain, true, but do not be a slave to your desires, rather let you be the elitist who controls your own actions, and splurge with common sense guiding you. Moderation is the key.

The military wastes an excessive amount of human and monetary resources that could best be put to policing and enforcing the drug war in this country. We don't need a larger amount of personnel. We need better precision of placement, military intelligence, and technology. Work smarter, not harder. Why not utilize our manpower in other ways, in outfitting our country with troops who are capable of multitasking? What gang banger in his right mind would stand up to even a minute fraction of our Marine Corps? If we did away with drug laws and treated drugs like other substances that are recreationally harmful to the self, we would need less money for police. With more civilians being armed and using their weapons responsibly, we would need police less and so they could focus on more serious crimes that the individual citizen need not be involved in.

If we stopped coddling our civilians, and forced them to take protection into their own hands, we would not have had the destruction of buildings, the loss of rescuers' lives, the funds to pay victims families, and the death toll in a foreign land, as well as $87 million in restoration of our enemies land, the injuries and loss of life aboard the two planes as well as below and inside the twin towers, from September 11th, 2001. People have been conditioned to not fight back even if it is for self-preservation because fighting of any kind is "wrong". This slows our reflexes down because we have to think about whether or not we should fight back. We have human instinct for a reason. Our instinct is to survive. Maybe if everyone on those planes, such as the heroes on Flight 93, had fought back fewer lives would have been lost.

We rebuilt Germany and Japan during the years after WWII. Need this country always do this? If I were to pull your chair out from under where you sit to read this and you beat me sensless for it, are you obligated to pay my hospital bills? I think not. I am responsible because it was my actions that caused the response. Cancel all debts to other lands and let the past be the past, but at the same moment, close our aid from then on, for if you give ten dollars to someone who has bothered you often and they disappear, never paying you back, it was money well spent because you never have to deal with them again! "God helps those who help themselves," the Christians love to say. Then live by it! Cease bailouts that take from my wallet and yours. Congress doesn't care. The Christian Apostle Paul said, "LET HE WHO DOES NOT SOW, LET HIM NOT EAT!" A plain, and yet very simple, statement of reason. Let the rich, bleeding heart individuals feed starving countries. If people are too ignorant to irrigate their crops after they have learned better methods, let them starve.

This is the very same group that supports forcing students to pledge allegiance in school by not overturning a ruling by a judge in a suit brought on by a parent. The suit was filed for a Pagan student's return to school after being expelled for refusing to pledge allegiance to "God" and the flag. This leads me to my fourth example of this countries flaws and how to go about fixing them. If we depict the Christian Ten Commandments in our government buildings, let us also put up the Koran, a giant sigil of Baphomet, a Venus of Willendorf, and a Buddha in every court room, thereby truly showing that this nation is land of the free and that we truly have freedom of religion. Put up symbols supporting all religions or simply put up nothing - showing that the government and the church truly are separate.

The United States Government as a whole needs to be revamped from the city council to the President himself. When you or I are hired to do a job we maintain that job based on work history and performance. Should our elected officials, such as Congress, be treated any different? Yet they are giving themselves raises from $63,500 to $92,000 merely from a vote conducted by themselves. If they are not doing their jobs then we should, by vote, fire those who do not keep their election promises. After investigation and trial, repossess their ill-gotten assets, disbursing them to the populace in the form of improving our zoos, our parks, our education and our health care.

This brings me to my final topic; the care of others. Just because I have halved the military, cut the national debt into pieces, and ended the cost of keeping inmates on death row, does not mean we are to spend more on those too lazy to get jobs to provide for themselves. Indeed, if we aid these people in a case-by-case basis (thereby creating more jobs) and help the destitute that flood our streets only while they seek work we will have more productive members of society and the system would be fairer. Those with children get help first, due to the fact that the children have weaker immune systems, have not been the cause of their own situation and are not able to provide for themselves. I know first hand that, once on the street, an adult can pull himself out of it with no help from the taxpayer.

We help those who need skills by having companies give grants to pay for those individual's education in a skill that would be valuable to that company. This way we weed out those who want to help themselves from those who sneer at working for a paycheck. It also helps establish loyalty to the company and increases economic stability if these people are then required to work for that company for a period of time once their education is complete.

Healthcare could advance greatly with all the funds confiscated from the old flawed judicial systems if allocated to curing many diseases and providing better hospitals. Health insurance raises the cost of our debts as individuals. The use of herbs could be implemented to cut costs as well as be more natural. If the church prior to the Dark ages had allowed the "wise ones" (the original meaning of the term "witch"), as well as medicine people from aboriginal sectors, to go untouched from the flames of heresy and, instead, had allowed then to flourish, we could have cured more ills than the last 100 years of modern science. But alas, our good friends in the times of Europe's inquisition nearly destroyed medicine from the Greeks as well as the

Druids. A healed man once wrote, "The witch did more good in one year than all these scripture men will do so long as they live…" Of course this may have a lot to do with the fact that the Black Plague nearly wiped out the old country completely, for in their haste to do "God's work", cats of any kind were killed (due to the fact they were believed to be the devil's minions and witches' familiars). The irony herein was that rats caused the plague itself, and without felines to kill them we see the results in history. It was common sense, cause and effect, not "God"'s punishment.

Healthcare would also be helped if we were to stop polluting the planet and destroying ourselves in the process. By putting these pollutants out into the atmosphere we are destroying the air we breathe, the food we eat (be it plant or animal) and the earth on which we live. How much sense does this make?

So there you have it, a better world to dwell in if a Satanist were to run things…

THE RISE AND FALL OF EMPIRES

It has been much lamented in our times that Christianity is suffering the wrath of the Pagan and Satanic communities. It has been said we should work together for an understanding, peaceful coexistence because "the fall of Christianity is the fall of Paganism." The more rights they lose, the more we lose ad nausea. Yes, I mean that. I am tired of the endless tirades and rhetoric of The Christian Right, the hypocrisy in news and politics. As a Satanist I enjoy the squirming of my enemies, and feel I must not let others forget the past.

The fires of the burning times should never be put out, for if we do not see the light of their embers indefinitely we will be likely to be torched again. It only takes a whisper of wind to stir up unthinkable flames of rage that can obliterate a group just because they are of another race, religion, or gender orientation.

In the Mediterranean a great Sumerian empire rose to power, the forerunner of all great civilizations, with every aspect of our current society. Greece and Rome had some of the most powerful of militaries of their day, evolved forms of government, and universities of staggering proportions thus paving the way for technology such as running water, aqueducts, flushing toilets and so much more. It gave us philosophers such as Socrates and Plato. The Aztecs of South

America, who were at their height when approached by Cortez, fell to Europe's power.

What is the point? They all had different religions, had power and fell, regardless of their former might or delusion's of longevity. Christian mythology has had it's

day for two millennia. If they fall from dominance, like they have done to countless other faiths, then that is the way of the world. Ancient races might call it poetic justice.

We as a world need to take off the rose colored glasses. If the prevailing thought is that all faiths united will prosper or suffer together, that by standing up for each other in a time of need you will win favors, think again. See how a paramedic at a Marilyn Manson concert watched the star pass out because of overexertion. The EMT applied the Hypocritic Oath, pardon me, the Hippocratic Oath, and denied him oxygen because the performer's lyrics had offended him! Should we repay it in kind? Not necessarily, but keep in mind, people do not always practice as their faith preaches. Tolerance goes both ways. We may never have the same courtesy in this land and quite possibly never will.

Service With A Smile

Ever been to a place of business and had less than stellar service? Take the majority of restaurants, for example. A place were one goes to unwind from a long hard day at work or taking care of kids, to enjoy good conversation and laugh a little while having our culinary needs taken care of without have to clean up afterward. We pay, with our hard earned money, for this service and for the food, not only to the establishment but also to the server for a job well done. Sadly, "a job well done" is becoming a rare occurrence. Nearly gone are the days when, in any eatery across the country, in any size city, you can find attentive help with a smile. Attentive means paying attention if your tables' glasses are less than half full and stopping by only once to find out if everything is alright instead of hovering and making the customer feel as if every mouthful is watched. At the finer dining establishments in major cities, or metropolises such as New York's Waldorf is, of course, a place where one would expect courteous treatment, par excellence. But are the average places the same? No.

Too often we, the customers, are remiss in our obligation to teach the server with our pocketbook the lessons of the past. Good service is rewarded with at least 20% of the check total. Some I notice however, tip without thinking, as if it is expected by societal standards to do so automatically. This honestly perplexes me to no end. If you received no return visit asking for water for example, or were given dirty cutlery repeatedly upon asking for clean, a red flag should be raised as to the worth of the business as a whole. Some time back I recall an episode of "Third Rock From the Sun," starring comedian Jonathan Lithgow, where he took a fellow campus staff member to dinner and began piling bills in a stack at his side of the table and a single dollar next to it. When asked what he was doing, he replied, "This pile is what the waiter could earn," pointing at the stack of bills, "and this is the pile they have earned," pointing to the single. He continued, "Each time I don't get what I want, I put a bill back on MY pile." Dramatic yes, but the point was made. Tips are not income by proxy, but earned wages. Incidentally, the reason we have the word "tips" is because it was an acronym that meant "To Insure Proper Service" as the tip was originally given at the beginning of a meal.

I travel a lot as a writer and dress for the occasion. Depending on the venue I speak at, I have dressed in a range of styles from a dark suit to antiquity Goth garb. Regardless, the attention to proper job performance should be observed, but this is not usually the case. The majority of the time, unless dressed up in modern business attire, I get less than satisfactory help. On the other hand, I have been to restaurants, been phenomenally well treated, and left a twenty dollar tip for a thirty dollar meal. When asked by the manager while paying the check how things were, I told the truth, and the waitress received a free steak dinner as well. Not only did she enjoy our praise, money and her food but I often went back to the same diner and requested her as my waitperson.

The other franchise, sadly, continues to lose my patronage due to rude help and patrons to match. It is loud, crowded, and would cause a newspaper critic to run screaming. Even worse are fast food establishments, where I have had to wait twenty minutes after paying the cashier and watched the drive through be served multiple times. The drive-thru, of course, had clocked tallies that report to corporate offices to impress where as the counter help could take as long as they liked and the corporation needn't know. A few scathing remarks to my companions, loud enough to be heard by the manager, finally got us our food. I never ate there again.

This type of behavior is not limited by any means to place we stop to eat. At nearly every multi-mart or mall one can imagine, I have no doubt, each of my readers can attest to a time where they have entered a store and workers either hounded them with questions while following their every move as if their faces were on *America's Most Wanted*. Then we have the other extreme where not a soul can be found for help. When you do finally find someone, they act indifferent to your queries as to products available other than what is in front of their noses. To suggest it may be backstocked, the indignant looks or sighs of discontent from the name tagged one implies the wait for their return from the warehouse in back may be indeed a long one. I myself have observed my coworkers, while stocking stores, stand in back chatting, never bothering to look, only to return to the "guest" and say said items were out of stock in shocking numbers.

Over my years of employment in the food industry, running several businesses, working in retail for over a decade and doing call center jobs, have had my managers marveling at my performance. I grew up in an age when manners were expected everywhere. Satanism stresses that we respect others when in the open, but also to treat others harshly when they deserve it. How to do so is the lingering question. Do we as customers have no options in dealing with this other than leaving our tables a mess or causing a scene? Not at all. Corporate offices have telephone numbers to reach them for complaints. If the management of these companies has a problem with giving you those contact numbers, online searches can yield results such as apology letters with free meal certificates, and sometimes the guilty party loses their job. With plenty of people out of work, there will always be someone waiting in the wings for a slacker's job. Fight back, with your wallet, voice and computer, until all that is left are the good ones. Then maybe we'll all get service with a smile.

Clothes DO Make the Man

It has been said "Clothing does not make the man". "Never judge a book by its cover". But why then do we, and does it not have some shred of validity?

Humans have the instinct to react when we come across something or someone. How we perceive it, and more importantly, how we choose to react to it are factors in this. Shock value is not the desired goal most often of course, but the dullards we exist among need a jolt from their collective mass of uniformity and lack of originality. People who flaunt being "alternative" by buying every stitch of clothing from Hot Topic amuse even the employees of the company. "You laugh at me because I'm different. I laugh at you because you're all the same," a shirt and sticker reads. An nonherdist sentiment, true, but when it gets taken to the extreme, going overboard in being what is constantly shifting as "alternative" is herdism and bowing gullibly to the corporate fascists. Instead of being "different" as these consumers believe themselves to be, they are all the same. Without realizing it they become walking contradictions at best and hypocrites at worse! If someone truly wishes to be different than everyone else, it is crucial to create your own look. You can do this by taken aspects from classic themes or anything else, while maintaining what uniquely makes you YOU. Respect others of course, but use caution and common sense. I like to wear long dark coats of many styles but with Columbine not so far off in some people's minds, a trench coat sends up warning signs, especially in warmer weather. Granted I may still do so, but I am well aware of the reaction I will get, depending on what else I wear with it.

I have tested this theory at malls while people watching out of the corner of my eye. I will, at whim, dress in leather and not shave. The next day or a short time later,

I will dress in a suit with my hair slicked back into a ponytail and walk into the same business. I usually get a totally opposite reaction, not to mention quicker assistance when dressed "normal". One instance of doing this I was followed, while wandering about the sporting goods department, with loss prevention tailing me in their oh so unnoticeable fashion, peering around corners. My roommate happened to be with me at the time, and was an employee at said store as well. He was stopped by the manager and grilled as to who I was and did he think I was a thief. Had I thought more of it at the time, a hefty lawsuit might have been the appropriate response in order to teach the manager how to better run his business.

I rarely, if ever, fail to get a job when I get interviewed. It is not only due to manners, skills, and a bit of wit, but I also dress or bathe as well or better than my interviewer. Many people forgo such amenities and show up at interviews with holes in their denim, tee shirts and various shoe types. Fine, if the job requires it, but how many do? We are judged by how we chose to look, and are treated accordingly. In the old days, a Satanist was described as a black, spiked leather jacketed, concert t-shirt wearing youth. The truth be known, most Satanists that I have had contact with wear dark suits with a slick but offsetting tie, such as blood red on a black dress shirt, or a black silk tie with flames on a dark shirt. A pin, ring or necklace of Baphomet usually goes with it, giving the appearance of a priest or businessman. There are times when it is necessary to shock people with the truth to shatter stereotypes. *The Satanic Witch* holds as much truth today on subjects such as heightening ones looks according to physical stature and personal appearance as it did years ago. Fashion may change a bit over the centuries, but aspects of what is professional and color accents change little. What is pleasing to the eye is a personal choice and, although aesthetics are subjective, there are universally given elements of harmonious configuration that are undeniably cohesive. People who wish to inspire others cultivate a certain look to attract others to them, be it either for the pleasure of their company or to command respect. Just as a male bird will have colorful plumage in order to attract a mate we will "dress up" when going out on the town. Women put on makeup and flattering clothing and men will fix their hair and wear appropriate attire in order to elicit positive responses from others.

Tailoring and maximizing classic styles of elegance does not block creativity or individuality by any means, in fact, it opens new doors by providing a wider expanse of choices and means to display your level of taste and class.

While walking with my good friend, Don Henrie, through my hometown late one night, we conversed about appearance and the public's reaction. Don is a prominent member of the Vampire subculture, and has been featured on Sci-Fi's Channel's *Mad Mad House* reality show, as well as *A&E Biography: Vampires*. We both agree that even if we opt to dress in clothing and jewelry of Gothic style, manners are important. "To be a leader, an Elder in the community, we have a responsibility to show how we are," says Don. This surprises the average person, and they remember. Good behavior from a "freak", in the eyes of the layperson, sticks even more in the recollections of the average person, more so than if we had been rude or sullen.

Rude behavior is a common misconception made about many within nocturnal circles. Being in our late twenties to early thirties but still being involved in what is mistakenly referred to as an adolescent's lifestyle, our polite conduct generates surprise in the general public. They hardly expect us to be courteous and well groomed. Shocking as it may be, professional appearance does indeed exist among the damned! How else do you explain the classic Devil in a tuxedo?

The majority of people I have interviewed or met since my first book was written, from Don Henrie and Michelle Belanger author of *The Psychic Vampire Codex* to artist Joseph Vargo of Monolith Graphics, and Satanist composer Le'Rue Delashay, have been some of the most wonderful, charming, and stunning looking people. Of course, not every person that is impeccably dressed is an outstanding human being but it does show good breeding, forethought and taste – a sign, at least from a distance, of promise compared to the average chap wandering the streets. Do the clothes themselves do it? No, of course not. But they, at times, reflect the wearer. We need to raise the bar for ourselves daily, let alone for those who would follow in our footsteps.

Hyde and Seek

Mr. Hyde. Frankenstein. Dracula. Phantom of the Opera... All of these names are infamous. We know them as monsters. They clearly have left an impression on the collective subconscious of man over the ages due to the underlying reminders that we too are as they, Nietzscheian creatures staring back at us from the abyss. These archetypes relate to aspects we find disturbing in ourselves.

It is easier to remove the unsettling taboo actions or wicked thoughts we all have and transpose it into such hideous caricatures. Fiction through the ages has been used to tell moral laden stories, wherein the villain, wearing black, was either hideous in appearance, by their deeds, or both. Yet we love them in spite of this or maybe more importantly, because of it. We root for the underdog sympathetically most likely because silently we wish we were the creature who does what he wishes for vengeance, power, or wealth.

Things we all wish for, to some degree or another, but rules of proper conduct prevent us from gaining. How we secretly hate it! We wish for the genie in the bottle, or for immortality. These figures offer that to us in escapism of books and in film.

Deeply dramatizing the dual nature of man is best presented in *The Strange Case of Dr. Jekyll and Mr. Hyde* (1886) by Robert Luis Stevenson. Having discovered the early draft of this story, his wife, horrified with what she read, hurled the ghastly manuscript into the fireplace. During a time of British technological advancement and leadership merging with the ideals of Western civilization, it was a commentary on living in a world of change outwardly as much as it was inwardly. Undaunted by his wife's prudish nature, and her fear of the realities of human nature he was attempting to express, Stevenson rewrote his classic of a scientist who discovers the unlocking of the minds hidden duality of life. The concoction transforms the mild Dr. Jekyll into a purely evil acting and thinking individual uninhibited in his wants, pursuing "undignified pleasures", murder, and various other sins. The mixture to reverse this proves too weak, and Hyde takes control until he is found dead by suicide, leaving a full confession. This story seeks to have the reader sympathize with the traumatized victim who attempts to shake off responsibility for his actions, denying the evil in himself; something similar to split personalities.

Comparable with the previous tale of mental trauma is Anne Rice's Vampire Chronicles where we find the character Louie. In Louie we find further examples of the struggle of these characters that are faced with choices and ramifications that conflict in their own minds. They desire to live two lives but are fearful of the results, complicated all the more by a strong dose of guilt. This signifies that desires are bad; the minimum price to pay is being ostracized. The character of Lestat, unlike Louie, embraced what he was and reveled in it. The common appeal of the archetype of vampires is the dual nature of a beautiful seducer which merges, seemingly paradoxically with that of a predator. Subconsciously we are drawn to what we fear. This is also seen in the "all good girls like the bad boy" archetype. The fear gets our blood boiling and provokes an almost primitive attraction.

The audience is fearful of the stages of depravity the lead character must endure in their transformation, and they eagerly cry 'foul' aloud while glued to the screen to see what happens next. In all such cases the hapless victims placed in the monsters' path are normal citizens, unwary and most often defenseless. Instead of feeling sorry for them, I cynically think to myself "They should have never crossed paths with the 'villain' in the first place!". These moral preaching classics attempt to lure the viewer into thinking that the struggle to gain knowledge and make use of powers that normal man cannot have (at least without selling their souls) is evil beyond redemption and the innocent 'victim' should be pitied. Consequences of disregarding morals leads one to tragic results – the dangers of acting as a sociopath, free of moral restraint, who they would have us believe needs be put down like a rabid dog.

Let us not forget the more simple fact that people go to see vampire movies because they like vampires! Most often in the classics, the monster had no choice in their condition.

We have religions and laws aplenty that dictate our actions, stifling our creative freedom by dictating what is acceptable, which causes guilt in healthy relationships sexually. The Marquis de Sade made a career telling tales of unrepressed urges taken to extremes. Labeled a monster in history as well as now, he nonetheless is devoured by his audiences through the passing decades. Is the Shadow that Jung spoke of evident here? Is the Marquis evil by bringing up hidden desires found in people, or is he just more able to articulate the thought suppressed by religious puritanical thought? Research shows that art and entertainment enhance life, not adversely affect it. If not, if such monsters and figures historically were not of some value for study, would they have gained the attention they have? It is important to take a close look at ourselves, to be healthy, regardless of guilt. In *Scream*, a cynical, almost satire poking fun of a large amount of horror movies, a lead character comments that the rule of survival in a horror film is to remain a virgin – clearly pointing out the classic horror movie statement that sex is evil, and the psycho is there to 'teach' a lesson – the modern Bogeyman who teaches children to behave.

With a gradual change in society's view of sex, it does however seem to have created the connotation that an appearance commonly accepted as attractive is a hero's necessary hallmark – the jock gets the girl in the end. In the 2004 film *The Phantom of the Opera*, the dashing and handsome Raoul is the stereotypical prince attempting to slay the dragon to save the princess. Like in *Frankenstein, the Modern Prometheus* it shows that despite the fact that the "creature" only wishes to be treated as an equal, superficiality prevails. How we react to the individual affects the victim and can induce them to change into the victimizer if they lash out, thus they become the monster and the average person is to be afraid. Does society not help to create them?

Erik, masked protagonist of the 1911 *Le Phantome de l'Opera* by Gaston Leroux, was much the same save for the fact he fully accepted what he was. The newer film, starring Gerard Butler, gave a poignant depiction of a horribly scarred man with the voice and passion of an angel who also possessed the fits of rage and unremorseful cold blooded killer. His decadent living quarters below the Opera house gave him harbor from the masses that would kill him for his hideous visage. His misanthropic nature was given birth by beatings and ridicule during childhood, and, fleeing a freak show after killing his abuser, he found peace in training the prodigal Christine.

The film tries to hint at stereotypical coloring of the "hero" versus the "villains" clothing and horses, but unlike the original black and white film starring Lon Chaney, it allows full expression of range and reason for his violent passions

– good and ill. We are left secretly rooting for the Phantom, well deserving, at least in part, of his vengeance. I also find some glee at the alternative ending from the original production where Lon Chaney's character was beaten to death by the angry mob. In this newer version, Butler's character survives and continues his love for the fair Christine. It is somewhat profound that this film symbolically starts in black and white, but shifts to color. A not so subtle reminder that the actions we do in the past are not easily thought of in simple terms of 'black and white'. Even Disney portrays this concept with Beauty and the Beast. In that movie the Beast shed his form after finding true love, thereby implying he need become 'attractive', in a commonly accepted sense, to be "normal" by the end of the tale. Such a good subliminal impression for children, suggesting anything not perfect is a curse, regardless of the type person within. I recognize that the "Beast" was changed into his "ugly" form because of his arrogance and vanity but could not Belle love him as she came to know him rather than him having to change back into the handsome prince?

Opposite this was the television show *Beauty and the Beast* starring Linda Hamilton and Ron Perlman. It was a favorite of mine when I was younger due to the fact I sympathized with Vincent, the "beast" character, being a creative, quiet and introspective youth, and found within him qualities that mirrored my own. He was a poet, I an artist. I also related to his feelings of distance from the rest of my peers. "I have seen your world. It has no place for me," he tells her, "I remind them of what they fear the most…. their aloneness." Most of the time, he cloaked himself in black hooded robes, preferring a candlelit sanctuary to read classic literature or pen his thoughts. He rarely left the subterranean labyrinth, observing normal people from a distant rooftop, feeling incapable of interaction due to stigma. His gentle nature was only given way to his rage when provoked by his beloved Catherine's life becoming threatened. In response, he gave full vent to his animalistic side. Vincent was a hero, a misunderstood loner that became a heartthrob of sorts to female viewers despite his looks. In this rare case, his nature mattered most.

Responsibility factor aside, let us examine the Columbine case briefly. I sympathize with the killers to a degree. Not because they were 'Goth loners' as the press mislabeled them, but because I was, as an adolescent, mercilessly tormented and beaten for being different. They did what I secretly wished to – they fought back without compunction. I carry some means of defense constantly, and, without a second's hesitation, would defend my life from attack. I simply choose not to go to the extreme of seeking out those who would harm me and striking preemptively. I unabashedly cheer for the antiheros, approving their slaughter in fiction. This is why comic books turned films warrant a cult like following. Nietzsche stated,

"The best and highest that men can acquire they must attain by crime". This leads one to think that only by ignoring the laws of man can we have our justice, regardless of the monster it makes us. In the 2006 release *V for Vendetta*, we have another anti-hero who, while also horribly scarred internally as well as externally, fights the system, conformity and the oppression of dogmatic dictatorship and maintains a love of beauty, creativity and freedom.

Frankenstein may lament his fate, wallowing in self-pity and sorrow that the world will not accept him, assuredly a 'woe is me' Goth sentiment. Satanically, I temper this reality by fully accepting my distance from the rest of the 'normal' world and embrace my darker nature more so in the fashion of Lestat, who spits in the eyes of god and revels in his decadent Byronic splendor, enjoying his power. His hidden pain is a passion and envy for life and the frailty of it as it passes by him in the form of some of the humans he encounters. Different perspectives are at work here. Accept how you are and make it a silver-lined cloud. I will walk that thin line because I see no other way.

How we are treated and how we choose to react will give us cause to ponder if we are a kind soul trapped in conflict of morality and our sense of making the wrong things right.

Acceptance of human nature and finding a balance is not so difficult a task if you are open minded enough to accept both aspects of ourselves instead of being in denial that we harbor the capacity for 'evil'. Responsibility and strong will to act with conviction are necessary elements for stability through the aftermath of circumstances that may arise. I leave you with the words of Machiavelli…

"Any man who tries to be good all the time is bound to come to ruin among the great number who are not good. Hence a prince who wants to keep his authority must learn how not to be good, and use that knowledge, or refrain from using it, as necessity requires."

So 'Hyde', if you need, from the realities of man's dual nature. Or 'seek' the truth.

Vlad, Rise of a Satanist

The true historical account of Vlad Tepes, otherwise known as Vlad the Impaler, who became the inspiration for Bram Stoker's novel *Dracula*, is portrayed well in the film *The Dark Prince*. It made no references to Vampires, though to the shrewd observer much of the fiction pointing to superstitious times (poor medical knowledge and psychosis) is somewhat obvious. I grew curious about the events and truths surrounding this man who later became such a key archetype. To further explore the life of this dark prince, I bought a copy of *Vlad the Impaler* by M.J. Trow and added much to my knowledge of vampire folklore. Some prominent events, actions by Tepes, and how he became demonized by popular misconception has echoed through time mirroring our modern day Church of Satan and its infamous founder. Long before Bram Stoker wrote his novel, the man known as Dracula (Vlad III) was the Voivod (prince) of Brasov of Walachia (Romania), and a member of the Ordu Dracul (in English, the Order of the Dragon) as was his father before him. The Order was an institution, similar to other chivalric orders of the time, modeled on the Order of St George (1318). The Holy Roman Emperor Sigmund, Vlad III's father, Vlad II, came to be known as Vlad Dracul because of his induction into the Ordu Dracul. "Dracul" means dragon and Vlad II came to be known as Vlad Dracul or Vlad the dragon. The "a" put on the end of the word "dracul" therefore signifies "son of" or "son of he who is a member of the Order of the Dragon" and is how Vlad III came to be known as Vlad Dracula. King of Hungary, and his queen mainly for the purpose of gaining protection for the royal family, established the

Order in 1408. According to its statute the Order also required its initiates to defend the cross and to do battle against its enemies, principally the Turks. The original Order comprised of twenty-four members of various noble families. In 1431 Sigmund summoned to the city of Nuremberg a number of princes and vassals useful for both political and military alliances. His primary objective was to initiate the group into the Order of the Dragon. One of these was Vlad Tepes[3] – a claimant for the throne of the principality of Walachia, who was at the time serving as commander guarding the mountain passes between

Transylvania and Walachia from enemy incursion. The Order of the Dragon adopted as its symbol the image of coats-of-arms of several noble families. For example, one class of the Order used a dragon being strangled with a cross draped across its back; another presents a cross perpendicular to a coiled dragon with an inscription "O quam misericors est Deus"[4] (vertical) and "Justus et paciens"[5] (horizontal). Other emblems of the Order included a necklace and seal, each with a variant form of the dragon motif. Vlad was obviously proud of this achievement. Later he had coins minted, which show on

[3]Pronounced tse-pesh in Romanian, it means "impaler" and was coined because of Vlad Dracula's penchant for impaling enemies on wooden poles.

[4]Translation – "Oh, how merciful God is" [5]Translation – "Justifiably and peacefully" one side a winged dragon. His personal coat-of-arms

also incorporated a dragon. Even to this day, the sword of the city of York has the Order's sigil on it. In all of these cases, the dragon was intended to convey a favorable image drawn from medieval iconography in which the dragon represented the Beast of Revelation who is slain by the forces of Christianity.

Once again the reference to the dragon was used as a term of honor, but soon the term Dracul gained the meaning of Devil, which was applied to members of the

Dracula family by their enemies and possibly also by superstitious peasants. Vlad continued to fight against the enemies of his land with cunning and viciousness, intent on persisting until it killed him. He did indeed die in battle, and his head was cut off and displayed in Istanbul by the sultan. His enemies in Turkey slandered him and the Catholic Church betrayed him. Vlad Dracula was not a vampire, but rumors throughout history have painted him far more evil than the forsaken blood drinker of Stoker's novel. Demonized as he was, as was Anton LaVey in the press equally centuries later, I find many parallels in historic figures maligned simply by living their lives to fulfillment on their own terms. According to a 1460 writer of papal transcripts, "untold abuses, sad murders, mutilations, and sorrows were visited upon Brasov by the unfaithful, cruel tyrant Dracula, who calls himself Vlad, prince... following the teachings of the Devil." Is this any different than the accusations made against the Church of Satan in the 1980's thru current times? Understandably, Vlad did indeed commit acts of harsh punishment, such as impalement, which he learned by example from the Ottoman Empire. He was forced to bear witness to such horrors as a child captive. Tortures such as he was accused of were often echoed by the Roman Catholic Church, committed upon faithful Christian crusaders such as The Templar Knights during the next hundred years. In my mind, this is exactly what LaVey says of personal attack in the Satanic Bible, "Hate your enemies with a whole heart, and if a man smites you on one cheek, SMASH him on the thigh! Self preservation is the highest law! Give blow for blow, scorn for scorn…eye for an eye, a tooth for tooth, aye four-fold, a hundred-fold! Make yourself a Terror of your adversary, and when he goeth his way, he will possess much additional wisdom to ruminate over. Thus you will make yourself more respected in all walks of life, your spirit – your immortal spirit – shall live, not an intangible paradise but in the brains and sinews of those whose respect you have gained." Tepes wished for all people in his land to be free of crime, no matter their social standing. He was said to have explained his actions by saying, "If someone lies or commits any injustice, he is not likely to stay alive, whether nobleman, priest, or common man. There must be security for all in my land." Such words are a historic example of a Satanist who lives by the Satanic Rule of the Earth, "When walking in open territory, bother no one. If someone bothers you, ask him to stop. If he does not stop, destroy him." Vlad's ideal, nearly utopian, society, within his own walls, is much like Lex Talionis.

Ironically, the people who he fought for eventually betrayed him. His was the first country during the Holy War to raise their banner against enemies of the cross. I am reminded of Baphomet in the history of the Templars, not long after the Crusades being rallied against by the Church as connected to the Devil. A distinct timeframe for occultists such as The Knights Templar and Mason's use of the goat headed figure that later would be synonymous with Crowley, (a LaVeyan influence) and most widely known as the Church of Satan's sigil. Coincidence or not?

It makes sense that many in the vampire culture revere this fictional and historical figure, for both have been misjudged as villains by those who are easily mislead, uneducated or simply too conservative to listen to reason. Vlad is still thought of as a national hero in Romania to this day, but history created a villain out of someone who would not conform to the rest of the world's sense of order.

In this way, Vlad was similar to today's youth with their dark and moody demeanor. I like to think of him as one of the world's first Satanists in a modern day sense.

NATURE AND MAN

The following is an excerpt from *Out of the Shadows* by John J. Coughlin, which I felt explained things from another perspective that seems to mirror mine.

"Nature is neither good nor evil; it simply is. It follows no moral code and has no internal motive. Only humans, with our complicated set of emotions and intellect, can justify such categorizations.

Death, destruction, chaos… these are essential driving forces within nature. Life feeds on life; destruction precedes creation. These are the only true laws, and they are not open to interpretation….It is our nature to fear the unknown. We cling to archetypal forms representing the aspects of some great unknowable, all-encompassing force, which we cannot comprehend. We call them our deities. This is not wrong; it is, in fact, necessary since we cannot easily grasp the 'divine' or cosmic source otherwise. Some religions choose to see this source as one omnipotent being. However, accepting the existence of an all-good and just being dictates that there must then exist a counterpart that encompasses evil. Pagans who think life is all happiness and joy and that once attuned to the rhythms of Nature, life become such wonderful dreams. Many subscribers to the 'New Age' movement have this shallow outlook: to them, nature is good and just and ordered. This simply is not the case. Take these dull-eyed individuals and place them in the wilderness with nothing but their crystals and they will be some animal's dinner before the end of the week. Nature is harsh. It is unforgiving. The weak die or are killed by the strong. Life feeds on life. Even the strictest vegan is a plant killer. Humans, with their technological and medical breakthroughs, have 'improved the quality life' by distancing themselves from the harshness of nature; softened us by removing us from nature's harsh reality.

However, despite this harsh side of nature, it is not evil. It also has its share of beauty. The point is, nature encompasses both creative and destructive forces.

Ignoring the negative aspects of anything most often results in an incomplete view of nature.

It is important to remember that focusing only on the darker side is just as dangerous as focusing only on the lighter side. Balance is important, and even though some may relate to one aspect more than the other, we must always remain open to the other aspects."

My own thoughts echo John's completely. The dark side of man is in his nature, regardless of a belief in Gods or Goddesses. The above is correct – we need balance within ourselves, to acknowledge that we are all capable of "good" or "evil." Survival of the fittest need not be simply psychical, or just the most intelligent. Again, balance. Uncommon sense, as I like to call it, is so rare that the herd automatically labels people and ideas into rigid patterns.

Once accepting the majority thought as "truth," no matter how absurd when carefully scrutinized, it becomes part of the mundane's lives. Those who speak of the beauty of nature rarely ever appreciate its "negative" aspects. They ignore the needed lessons constantly presented to them, meandering aimlessly through life never fully enjoying what is right before them!

We each have within us the burning source of motivation, to pursue truth, knowledge, power and pleasure. Pervasive discontent cannot be eliminated by avoiding it. It must be embraced and made to be our servant. We must never allow doubt or fear hold us back from triumph.

Nature does not give mercy nor offer a second chance…yet indeed it does flourish. We can learn a lot from both nature and that which dwells alongside we adults, as reminders of how else to be – animals and children. LaVey gave full vent to his joys, and rages and often said the nature of man was reflected in both. Seeing the world for what it is instead of blindly accepting rules of society, religion or anything else that would cause us to hold ourselves back from questioning the limits to the heights of our potential. This, above all else, is the hallmark of Satanism, from Faust to LaVey as models of Satanic virtue.

Misplaced 'Alien Elite'

The feeling of being 'not like' everyone else was one of puzzlement to me as a child. I felt both out of touch with my peers, as I was not into things like sports, preferring instead to read. I watched people a lot to understand this great divide I felt between them and I. Eventually I simply shrugged it off a fluke, or it is what it is. As I grew older the rift seemed to widen. I prefer wine to anything remotely like beer, I like old world architecture, heavy Baroque framed mirrors, wood floors – indeed, wood unpainted but stained and carved for a home would be fantastic, an old styled manor is my dream house, something along the lines of those found on (historicproperties.com), the Carleton Villa or any number of stone mausoleums! It seems to me that old world aesthetics are a thing of the past, or only the wealthy can create or buy them in Europe.

My likes were for other things, fashions of bygone eras, fro Luis the XIV, to the Edwardian Period and the Gangster Era. I have always felt out of my time period and any one of those would suit me better. In those days, and artist or writer was a person of great respect, indeed the only way to make something of oneself outside of war or being born into wealth. To this day, I dress as nice as my professors (or better) and am asked frequently if I am a teacher at my college. I believe very strongly we do ritual on a subconscious daily basis. We create who we are, and also create the person we are to be by positive reinforcement. By careful selection of wardrobe, colors and projection of determination we 'become' something bigger. I light my room by candle light to create a mood, burn incense and drape my walls with fabric to transform my creative space. It is my goal in life to completely create my own style in everything I own, create and present myself as. When it comes to suits, they are clean, dark and classic solid colors for the shirts. I hate collars and cuffs that don't match the shirt; I love cufflinks as they are old styled and true taste in finer things. Cut crystal stem ware has always held my eye, and I enjoy decorating my abode with wall to wall bookcases, hard wood floors, art in heavy carved frames and stone fireplaces. Even though I am approaching middle age I try to get some exercise in every few days, to balance my long hours in writing at my desk. I paint and go shooting as a stress relief (or just for the fun of it!) Personally, if you have a sense of self and a harmonious, balanced sense of aesthetics it isn't that hard to turn average in to beautiful with a little work. I painted an entire house, redid floors, and hung fabrics from the walls to build a total environment of my own making. We constantly are bombarded with other people's whims, smells, colors and fashion sense so it only seems logical to me to have a near obsessive interior decorating skill and being OCD about color and balance of objects (this also comes from being an artist) as a necessary counter balance to it all. Of course, the library is full of books I have actually read or will soon, selected from lengthy wish lists collected while browsing bookstores and Amazon.

This may seem odd to most people, but consider the fact when the average person in Europe is asked what they think of when of your average American, they said *Homer Simpson*. That's right, a cartoon figure who is fat, lazy drunk, stupid beyond relief and a poor father to his children! Too often people are of extremes in personality, either working far too hard or being totally apathetic and lazy! Given the choice of consequences, I much prefer to be a workaholic to spoil myself with nice things than allow myself to get so frustrated I give up pushing because it is too much work. There is no harm in spending money on the finer things as long as one is not so stupid they do not pay bills, take care of their children, etc. But I am also patient while saving for those things. When tax returns come along or extra money from grants while in college I used it responsibly but always, every year get one or two things to reward myself for being both patient and selected something I wanted carefully. It didn't matter if it was a nice suit, a high quality gun for the collection or a piece of furniture of electronics. Pay yourself is the idea, and treat yourself well. I have come to realize that if you truly appreciate yourself (and no one else will, ever, to the level you want to be treated) you have to take the steps to make it happen.

When you come to a point in life where you look at yourself in the mirror after looking out at the mass of people while taking in the crowd outside are you happy being you or would you rather be a unique individual no matter how out of the ordinary you may seem to be to others?

Not My Glass

Ever wonder what to do when someone bothers you with his or her unrelenting tirades, endless chatter, and personal woes, ad nauseum.

Often I find myself appreciating the silence of my bedchamber, an aesthetically pleasant environment, to contemplate various matters of philosophical importance, and thoughts of magical/spiritual debate, or a variety of socially deviant activities. I am not suggesting we all become hermits. I'm stating that we should simply enjoy a moment's reprieve from the humdrum of work and the drone of the idiot box, as I refer to the family altar, the television. I have more to do with my life than debate fools on how they perceive their particular worldview. My time could be better spent drawing or painting in my art studio, holding an intellectual conversation with a few good friends discussing Plato, Socrates, and the writings of Nietzsche or Jung.

On occasion, however, I will take time out at work, while being bored, to engage in a lively debate of "wits" with those that are hopelessly outgunned. It accomplishes many things. One, it wastes time while I have little choice but to be there. Two, it clearly proves to me that people as a whole are less bright than I feel they should be, and it clearly states for all observing who is the more intelligent in the group, placing them in their proper spot on the intellectual food chain. For an example of this, and why I see my coworkers as I do, take a look at my article *Would You Like Fries With That?*

You might at this point be wondering why I chose the title I have for my article. It is because I am suggesting the age old question psychologists ask; "Is the glass half empty or half full?" has three possible answers, not two.

We are expected by society's programming (in many aspects of life) to think only within the given parameters of acceptable questions and answers, instead of challenging the challengers with questions back, opening them and yourself to the possibility of greater than typical regurgitations of the thoughts of someone else. This is thinking outside the box.

To ponder a question that allows only two answers, while both are valid, is ludicrous except in an effort to discern how one perceives life overall. Are you an optimist or a pessimist? I debated this with a coworker one day who gave me an answer to not only the personality question, but also what to do with the above mentioned annoying people, to wit he replied, "I don't give a shit. It's NOT MY GLASS." Profound wisdom from someone whose thoughts generally abound with getting drunk, watching sports, and ogling girls young enough to date his son.

I feel this reply to be an evolvement of true perception and it throws off the person asking you such an inane question. Logic says, if it were your glass, the level of liquid therein would be obvious as well as HOW it came to be that way. If you poured it or consumed it, it is a matter of how full did you make it from either the top or bottom.

IF, however, it is not your glass in the first place, why should you be concerned with its level? This is a waste of your time, as well as the time you or I would feel was wasted on listening to others' problems, gossip, etc. that you would find irrelevant to your life. This does not apply to enlightened talk among friends, as an exercise of the mind. I hope I have given you a fresh perspective as well as encouraging everyone who reads this to not give an automatic, mechanically expected answer. If you have gained nothing from this, "It's not my glass."

About the Author

E.R. Vernor, 'an author, publisher and lecturer who has written over two dozen books on popular culture. The content ranges from vampires and zombies to the Devil and the occult. He has also been a consultant for A&E Channel's Paranormal State. He has appeared as a repeated guest speaker at Dragon Con, Scarefest, Parafest, and Dead Con He has been interviewed on the BET Channel's The Lexi Show episode "The Church of Satan".

NOTED INDIVIDUALS

Alexander the Great

(July, 356 BC,- June 10, 323 BC)

Alexander was born in Pella, Macedon, King of Macedon during 336–323 BC, is considered one of the most successful military commanders in world history, conquering most of the known world before his death. His conquests ushered in centuries of Greek settlement and rule over foreign areas, a period known as the Hellenistic Age. Alexander himself lived on in the history and myth of both Greek and non-Greek cultures. Already during his lifetime, and especially after his death, his exploits inspired a literary tradition in which he appears as a towering legendary hero in the tradition of Achilles.

Aristotle

(384 BC – March 7, 322 BC)

Aristotle was an ancient Greek philosopher, student of Plato and teacher of Alexander the Great. He wrote books on many subjects, including physics, poetry, zoology, logic, rhetoric, government, and biology. Along with Plato and Socrates, is generally considered one of the most influential of ancient Greek philosophers. They transformed Pre-Socratic Greek philosophy into the foundations of Western philosophy as we know it. The writings of Plato and Aristotle form the core of Ancient philosophy. Aristotle valued knowledge gained from the senses and in modern terms would be classed among the modern empiricists. He is known for being one of the few figures in history who studied almost every subject possible at the time. In science, Aristotle studied anatomy, astronomy, economics, embryology, geography, geology, meteorology, physics, and zoology. In philosophy, Aristotle wrote on aesthetics, ethics, government, metaphysics, politics, psychology, rhetoric and theology. He also dealt with education, foreign customs, literature and poetry. His combined works practically constitute an encyclopedia of Greek knowledge.

Byron, George Gordon (Noel), 6th Baron

(January 22, 1788–April 19, 1824)

Lord Byron was an Anglo-Scottish poet and leading figure in Romanticism. Among his best-known works are the narrative poems Childe Harold's Pilgrimage and Don Juan. The latter remained incomplete on his death.

Byron's fame rests not only on his writings, but also on his life, which featured extravagant living, numerous love affairs, debts, separation, allegations of incest and sodomy and an eventual death from fever after he travelled to fight on the Greek side in the Greek War of Independence. He was famously described by Lady Caroline Lamb as "mad, bad, and dangerous to know."

Goethe, Johann Wolfgang von

(28 August 1749 – 22 March 1832)

Goethe was a German novelist, dramatist, poet, humanist, scientist, philosopher, and for ten years chief minister of state at Weimar.

Goethe was one of the paramount figures of German literature and European Neo-classicism and Romanticism in the late 18th and early 19th centuries. The author of Faust and Theory of Colours, he inspired Darwin with his independent discovery of the human premaxilla jaw bones and focus on evolution. Goethe's influence spread across Europe, and for the next century his works were a primary source of inspiration in music, drama, and poetry.

de Sade, The Marquis

(June 2, 1740 – December 2, 1814)

Donatien Alphonse François de Sade, better known as the Marquis de Sade and nicknamed the Divine Marquis), was a French aristocrat and writer of philosophy-laden and often violent pornography, as well as some strictly philosophical works. His is a philosophy of extreme freedom, unrestrained by ethics, religion or law, with the egotistical pursuit of personal pleasure being the highest principle. Much of his writing was done during the 29 years he was incarcerated.

Machiavelli, Niccolo

(May 3, 1469-June 21, 1527)

Niccolo Machiavelli was a Florentine political philosopher, musician, poet, and romantic comedic playwright. Machiavelli was also a key figure in realist political theory, crucial to European statecraft during the Renaissance. Machiavellianism is the term some social and personality psychologists use to describe a person's tendency to deceive and manipulate the others for personal gain. Used to describe later works by other authors based on Machiavelli's writings – particularly The Prince – in which the authors stress the view that "The ends justify the means." These authors failed to include some of the more moderating themes found in Machiavelli's works and the name is now associated with the extreme view point.

Mencken , Henry Louis

(September 12, 1880 – January 29, 1956)

Better known as H. L. Mencken, was a twentieth century journalist, satirist and social critic, a cynic and a freethinker, known as the "Sage of Baltimore" and the "American Nietzsche". He is often regarded as one of the most influential American writers of the early 20th century. At one point in his career he was America's favorite pundit and literary critic at the same time. Mencken was an outspoken defender of freedom of conscience and civil rights, an opponent of persecution and of injustice and of the Puritanism and self-righteousness that masks the oppressive impulse. As a nationally syndicated columnist and author of numerous books he notably assaulted America's preoccupation with fundamentalist Christianity, and was labeled a misogynist.

Nietzsch , Friedrich Wilhelm

(October 15, 1844 – August 25, 1900)

Nietzsche was a German philosopher, whose critiques of contemporary culture, religion, and philosophy centered around a basic question regarding the foundation of values and morality. Beyond the unique themes dealt with in his works, Nietzsche's powerful style and subtle approach are distinguishing features of his writings. Although largely overlooked during his short working life, which ended with a mental collapse at the age of 44, and frequently misunderstood and misrepresented thereafter, Nietzsche received recognition during the second half of the 20th century as a highly significant figure in modern philosophy. His influence was particularly noted throughout the 20th century by many existentialist, phenomenological and postmodern philosophers, including Anton LaVey on concepts of Apollonian-Dionysian Duality, Eternal Recurrence, Will to Power, Nihilism, Herd Instinct, Overman, Attack on Christianity, Master-Slave Morality.

Paine, Thomas

(January 29, 1737 – June 8, 1809)

An intellectual, scholar, revolutionary, and idealist, is widely recognized as one of the Founding Fathers of the United States. A radical pamphleteer, Paine anticipated and helped foment the American Revolution through his powerful writings, most notably Common Sense, an incendiary pamphlet advocating independence from Great Britain. An advocate for classical liberalism - a philosophy shared by most of the founding fathers, resembling modern Libertarian ideals of small government, personal freedom and free markets and constitutional republican government, he outlined his political philosophy in The Rights of Man, written both as a reply to Edmund Burke's view of the French Revolution and as a general political philosophy treatise as well as Common Sense, a treatese on the benefits of personal liberty and limited government, in which he considers society a representation of human ideals, and government a necessary evil. Paine was also noteworthy for his support of deism, taking its form in his treatise on religion The Age of Reason.

Shelley, Percy Bysshe

(August 4, 1792 – July 8, 1822)

Percy Shelly was one of the major English romantic poets, widely considered to be among the finest lyric poets in the English language. He is perhaps most famous for such anthology pieces as Ozymandias, Ode to the West Wind, To a Skylark, and The Masque of Anarchy; but his major works were long visionary poems such as Adonais and Prometheus Unbound. Shelley's unconventional life and uncompromising idealism made him a notorious and much denigrated figure in his own life, but he became the idol of the following two or three generations of poets (including the major Victorian poets Robert Browning, Alfred Tennyson, Dante Gabriel Rossetti and Algernon Charles Swinburne, as well as William Butler Yeats). He was also famous for his association with contemporaries John Keats and Lord Byron, and, like them, for his untimely death at a young age. He was married to the famous novelist Mary Shelley, author of Frankenstein.

Spencer, Herbert

(27 April 1820 – 8 December 1903)

An English philosopher and prominent liberal political theorist. Although today he is chiefly remembered as the father of Social Darwinism, a school of thought that applied the evolutionist theory of survival of the fittest (a phrase coined by Spencer) to human societies, he also contributed to a wide range of subjects, including ethics, metaphysics, religion, politics, rhetoric, biology and psychology. He was a close contemporary of many famous philosophers and scientists of his period such as John Stuart Mill, Thomas Huxley and Charles Darwin and was renowned for the long-reaching, accessible, and profoundly sensible qualities of his work. Although he has often been criticized as a perfect example of scientism, he was at the time considered by many to be one of the most brilliant men of his generation.

Wollstonecraft Shelley Godwin, Mary

(August 30, 1797 – February 1, 1851)

Mary Shelley was an English novelist who is perhaps equally famous as the wife of Romantic poet Percy Bysshe Shelley and as the author of Frankenstein, or The Modern Prometheus. Mary was born in London, England, the second daughter of famed feminist, educator and writer Mary Wollstonecraft and the equally famous liberal philosopher, anarchic journalist and atheist dissenter, William Godwin. Mary Shelley died of brain cancer on February 1, 1851 in London and was interred at St. Peter's Churchyard in Bournemouth, in the English county of Dorset. At the time of her death, she was a recognized novelist.

Heidegger, Martin

(September 26, 1889 – May 26, 1976)

Heidegger was a German philosopher. He influenced many other major philosophers, and his own students at various times included Hans-Georg Gadamer, Hans Jonas, Emmanuel Levinas, Hannah Arendt, Xavier Zubiri and Karl Löwith. Maurice Merleau-Ponty, Jean-Paul Sartre, Jacques Derrida, Michel Foucault, Jean-Luc Nancy, and Philippe Lacoue-Labarthe also studied his work more or less closely. Beyond his relation to phenomenology, Heidegger is regarded as a major or indispensable influence on existentialism, deconstruction, hermeneutics and postmodernism. He attempted to reorient Western philosophy away from metaphysical and epistemological and toward ontological questions, that is, questions concerning the meaning of being, or what it means to be.

Carl Gustav Jung

July 26, 1875 – June 6 1961

Swiss psychiatrist and founder of Analytical Psychology. C. G. Jung's unique and broadly influential approach to psychology emphasized understanding the psyche through exploring the worlds of dreams, art, mythology, world religion and philosophy. Though not the first to analyze dreams, he has become perhaps the most well known pioneer in the field of dream analysis. Although he was a theoretical psychologist and practicing clinician for most of his life, much of his life's work was spent exploring other realms: Eastern vs. Western philosophy, alchemy, astrology, sociology, as well as literature and the arts. Jung also emphasized the importance of balance. He cautioned that modern humans rely too heavily on science and logic and would benefit from integrating spirituality and appreciation of the unconscious realm. Interestingly, Jungian ideas are not typically included in curriculum of most major universities' psychology departments, but are occasionally explored in humanities departments.

Many pioneering psychological concepts were originally

proposed by Jung, such as the Collective subconscious and

Archetypes.

LaVey, Anton Szandor

(1930—1997)

LaVey was the founder of the Church of Satan He became well-versed in the many rackets used to separate the rubes from their money, along with the psychology that lead people to such pursuits. He played music for the bawdy shows on Saturday nights, as well as for tent revivalists on Sunday mornings, seeing many of the same people attending both. LaVey worked for awhile as a photographer for the Police Department, and, during the Korean War, enrolled in San Francisco City College as criminology major.

(Condensed from facts found on the website www.churchofsatan.com, written by High Priest Peter Gilmore, Church of Satan.)

Ayn Rand

February 2 1905 – March 6, 1982

Born Alissa Zinovievna Rosenbaum, was best known for her philosophy of Objectivism and her novels We the Living, Anthem, The Fountainhead, and Atlas Shrugged. Her philosophy and her fiction both emphasize, above all, the concepts of individualism, rational egoism ("rational self-interest"), and capitalism, which she believed should be implemented fully via Laissez-faire capitalism. Her politics has been described as minarchism and libertarianism, though she never used the first term and detested the second.

Her novels were based upon the projection of the Randian hero, a man whose ability and independence causes conflict with the masses, but who perseveres nevertheless to achieve his values. Rand viewed this hero as the ideal, and the express goal of her fiction was to showcase such heroes.

Wagner, Wilhelm Richard

(May 22, 1813 in Leipzig – February 13, 1883 in Venice)

Richard Wagner was an influential German composer, conductor, music theorist, and essayist, primarily known for his groundbreaking symphonic-operas (or "music dramas"). His compositions are notable for their continuous contrapuntal texture, rich harmonies and orchestration, and elaborate use of leitmotifs: themes associated with specific characters or situations. Wagner's chromatic musical language prefigured later developments in European classical music, including extreme chromaticism and atonality. He transformed musical thought through his idea of Gesamtkunstwerk ("total art-work"), epitomized by his monumental four-opera cycle Der Ring des Nibelungen (1876). His concept of leitmotif and integrated musical expression was a strong influence on many 20th century film scores. Wagner is also a controversial figure, both for his musical and dramatic innovations.

Wilde, Oscar Fingal O'Flahertie Wills

(October 16, 1854 – November 30, 1900)

Wilde was an Anglo-Irish playwright, novelist, poet, and short story writer. One of the most successful playwrights of late Victorian London, and one of the greatest celebrities of his day, known for his barbed and clever wit, he suffered a dramatic downfall and was imprisoned after being convicted in a famous trial of "gross indecency" for homosexual acts.

Recommended Reading

The Death and Life of Philosophy, St. Augustine's Press (April 1, 1999)

The 48 Laws of Power, Penguin (September 1, 2000) By Robert Greene

The Art of Seduction, Penguin; Reprint edition (October 7, 2003) By Robert Greene

The 35 Strategies of War, Viking Adult (January 19, 2006) By Robert Greene

The Dark Side of Christian History, Morningstar Books (July 1, 1995) By Helen Ellerbe

Philosophy of Humanism, Ungar Publishing, 01 January, 1974 By Corliss Lamont

The Book Your Church Doesn't Want You to Read, By Tim C. Leedom

Truth Seeker, Reprint edition (September 1, 2001)

The Christ Conspiracy: The Greatest Story Ever Sold. By Acharya S Adventures Unlimited Press (September 1, 1999)

Forbidden Knowledge: From Prometheus to Pornography, Harvest Books; Reprint edition (September 15, 1997) By Roger Shattuck

The Prince, Penguin Classics, 1998 Florentine Histories, new translation. Introduction by Harvey Mansfield, Jr., Princeton University Press (August 3, 1990) By Niccolò Machiavelli

The Art of War, Da Capo Press (September 4, 2001)

Philosophy - who needs it, Signet Book (November, 1984) By Ayn Rand

Atlas Shrugged, Signet Book; 35th Anniversary edition (August 1996) By Ayn Rand

The Birth of Tragedy, 1872 in: 'Basic Writings of Nietzsche', trans. Walter Kaufmann, Modern Library, 2000 By Friedrich Nietzsche

The Birth of Tragedy and the Case of Wagner', trans. Walter Kaufmann, Vintage, 1967

The Birth of Tragedy & the Genealogy of Morals, trans. Francis Golffing, Anchor Books, 1956

The Untimely Meditations, 1873-6, in *Unfashionable Observations*, trans. Richard T. Gray, Stanford University Press, 1998

Human, All Too Human, 1878, trans. R. J. Hollingdale, Cambridge University Press, 1996

The Dawn, 1881, in: 'Daybreak', trans. R. J. Hollingdale, Cambridge University Press, 1997

The Gay Science, 1882, 1887, trans. Walter Kaufmann, Vintage, 1974

Thus Spoke Zarathustra, 1883-5, in: 'The Portable Nietzsche', trans. Walter Kaufmann, Penguin, 1977

Beyond Good and Evil, 1886, in: *'Basic Writings of Nietzsche'*, trans. Walter Kaufmann, Modern Library, 2000

On the Genealogy of Morals, 1887, in: *'Basic Writings of Nietzsche'*, trans. Walter Kaufmann, Modern Library, 2000

and in: *The Birth of Tragedy & the Genealogy of Morals*, trans. Francis Golffing, Anchor Books, 1956

The Case of Wagner, 1888, in: *'Basic Writings of Nietzsche'*, trans. Walter Kaufmann, Modern Library, 2000

Twilight of the Idols, 1888, in: *'The Portable Nietzsche'*, trans. Walter Kaufmann, Penguin, 1977

The Antichrist, 1888, in: *'The Portable Nietzsche'*, trans. Walter Kaufmann, Penguin, 1977

Ecce Homo, 1888, in: *'Basic Writings of Nietzsche'*, trans. Walter Kaufmann, Modern Library, 2000

Nietzsche contra Wagner, 1888, in: *'The Portable Nietzsche'*, trans. Walter Kaufmann, Penguin, 1977

The Will to Power and Other Posthumous Collections, ed. and trans. Walter Kaufmann, Vintage, 1968.

Writings from the Late Notebooks, ed. Rüdiger Bittner, Cambridge University Press, 2003.

Philosophy and Truth: Selections from Nietzsche's Notebooks of the Early 1870s, ed. and trans. Daniel Breazeale, Prometheus Books, 1990.

Philosophy in the Tragic Age of the Greeks, trans. Marianne Cowan, Regnery Publishing, 1996.

The Pre-Platonic Philosophers, trans. Greg Whitlock, University of Illinois Press, 2001

The Satanic Bible, Avon; Reissue edition (December 1, 1976) By Anton Szandor LaVey

Satanic Rituals, Avon; Reissue edition (December 1, 1976) By Anton Szandor LaVey

The Satanic Witch, Feral House; 2nd edition (March 1, 2003) By Anton Szandor LaVey

Satan Speaks! Feral House (September 1, 1998) By Anton Szandor LaVey

The Devil's Notebook, Feral House (November 1, 1992) By Anton Szandor LaVey

The Church of Satan: A History of the World's Most Notorious Religion, Hell's Kitchen Productions Inc (November 1, 1990) By Blanche Barton

Secret Life of a Satanist: The Authorized Biography of Anton LaVey, Feral House (September 1, 1992)

PUBLICATIONS BY CHURCH OF SATAN MEMBERS

The Black Flame, the International Forum of the Church of Satan, Hells Kitchen P.O.Box 499 Radio City Station, New York, NY 10101-0499.

The Cloven Hoof, the official Bulletin and Tribunal of the Church of Satan PMB # 365, P.O.Box 390009 San Diego, CA 92149-0009

Not like Most, A Publication of Satanism In Action, by Magister Matt G. Paradise. Purging Talon Publishing, P.O.Box 8131 Burlington, Vermont, 05402

The Ninth Gate Magazine, P.O. Box 11496 Fort Wayne, IN 46858 Warlock Nocturnum

The Trident, Published by 3-Tine Productions, Legion of Loki, P.O.Box 140252 St. Louis, MO 63114 www.3tine.com.

Lust Magazine, by Warlock Jack Malenche and Shiva Rodriguez. Sexuality explored in all its consensual forms. www.sataniclust.com.

The Black Pun-Kin, Canada's leading Satanic publication, by Magister Robert A. Lang. P.O. Box 32017, 1386 Richmond Road, Ottawa, ON, Canada K2B 1A1

Scapegoat, P.O.Box 381198, Hollywood, CA, 900038-1198.

The Dark Corner, Finland's debut Satanic magazine.

The Devil's Diary, Reverend Blackthorne's magazine of news, reviews and essays.

Rule Satannia, Full color magazine, full of news and great articles. Heldon Press, P.O. Box, 27, Drakes Broughton, Pershore, WR10WB/ United Kingdom.

www.rulesatannia.com.

Conquer Now, Satanic magazine.

Eyes Only, created by and for Satanists, a magazine newsletter looking out for the misanthrope's best interests.

P.O. Box 1339, New York, NY 10159-1339.

The Yin Conductor, publication of the Alien Elite, by Lu Hutchinson. 1255 N.th St., Laramie, WY 82070.

Diabolical Diatribes, by Paul Dunphy, P.O. Box 354, Troy NY, 12182.

The Raven, N.B. Smith's *"Satanic Journal of Humor and Good Living – the Lighter Side of the Dark Side"* P.O. Box 482, Stratford, CT 06615-0482

Books by Church of Satan Members

Embracing the Darkness; Understanding Dark Subcultures, by Corvis Nocturnum, Dark Moon Press (May 1, 2005)

Satanic Scriptures, by Peter H. Gilmore Scapegoat Publishing

Bearing the Devils Mark, by Matt G. Paradise, Purging Talon Publishing, P.O.Box 8131 Burlington, Vermont, 05402

Essays in Satanism, by James D. Sass

The Pseudo-Satanist Bible, by Reverend K.S. Anthony.

Might is Right - The Survival of the Fittest, by Ragnar Redbeard, published by EvilNOW.com, Bugbee Books

Satan Wants You: The Cult of Devil Worship in America by Arthur Lyons, Mysterious Press (June 1, 1988)

Lucifer Rising: Sin, Devil Worship, and Rock'n'Roll by Gavin Baddeley, Plexus Publishing; 2nd edition (January 9, 2006)

Lords of Chaos: The Bloody Rise of the Satanic Metal Underground by Michael Moynihan and Didrik Søderlind, Feral House (December 1, 2003)

Claw and Fang, by Colonel Akula. A self defense book by combat expert and author.

Sacred Hunger, Dark Moon Press (January 1, 2005) By J. Gordon Melton

Vampire Book: The Encyclopedia of the Undead Visible Ink Press; 2nd edition (December 1, 1998)

By *Radu Florescu*, Raymond T. McNally

In Search of Dracula: The History of Dracula and Vampires, Houghton Mifflin; Revised edition (October 31, 1994)

Dracula, Prince of Many Faces: His Life and His Times, Back Bay Books; 1st edition (October 31, 1990) By M. J. Trow

Vlad the Impaler: In Search of the Real Dracula, Sutton Publishing (July 1, 2004)

By Barbara Knox

www.ingramcontent.com/pod-product-compliance
Lightning Source LLC
Chambersburg PA
CBHW060133100426
42744CB00007B/769